In Chinese culture, asking "Are you hungry?" is more than a question—it's a way of showing you care. It's the love language Ming-Na Wen grew up with in Pittsburgh, where her parents ran the iconic Chinatown Inn restaurant. While many fans know her as the legendary, award-winning actress behind Disney's *Mulan* or Fennec Shand in the *Star Wars* franchise, off the screen, Ming-Na is also legendary in the kitchen, cooking traditional Chinese dishes for her family and friends.

Have You Eaten Yet? brings that same warmth to her fans, offering approachable and delicious recipes inspired by her family, heritage, and restaurant roots. In chapters like Restaurant Classics, you'll learn to master iconic dishes such as The Best Egg Rolls, Simple Wonton Soup, and Shrimp Fried Rice. Discover family secrets from her father in Feasts from Chef Baba, with recipes including his tender Prime Rib and comforting Winter Melon Soup. Straight from Ming-Na's Kitchen, you'll find crowd-pleasers such as Shrimp with Garlic Noodles and the showstopping Dragon Fruit Cheesecake Cups. Ming-Na even shares her secrets for making perfect rice, conquering condiments, and prepping sauces, broths, and dry spices like a restaurant pro.

Filled with personal stories, heartwarming memories, practical tips, and never-before-seen family photos, *Have You Eaten Yet?* is an essential guide for anyone looking to explore the rich flavors of Chinese American cuisine.

Have You Eaten Yet?

Have You Eaten Yet?

吃飯了嗎？

FAMILY RECIPES FROM A RESTAURANT DAUGHTER

Ming-Na Wen

with **Ann Volkwein**

Photography by **Jennifer Chong**

SIMON ELEMENT

New York Amsterdam/Antwerp London
Toronto Sydney/Melbourne New Delhi

FOR BABA AND MOMMY, WHO SHARED THEIR LOVE THROUGH EVERY DISH THEY MADE. AND FOR ERIC, MICHAELA, AND COOPER, WHO ARE MY EVERYTHING IN EVERY WAY.

CONTENTS

FEASTS FROM CHEF BABA

MING-NA'S KITCHEN

PANTRY FUNDAMENTALS

INTRODUCTION

In Chinese culture, when someone asks "Are you hungry?" or "Have you eaten?" it's more than just a question about food—it's a way of saying hello. It's a gesture of connection. It's a way of showing that we care.

For me, love has always been tied to food—my memories are deliciously streaked with heaping plates of beef chow fun and delicate steamed fish with ginger and scallions. You see, I had the great privilege of being a restaurant daughter, growing up in the (still open!) Chinatown Inn in Pittsburgh, which my parents owned. I had two amazing chefs as parents. Every night, my mom and dad would cook five-course dinners for my brothers and me. (Yes, you read that right—five!) Like many traditional Chinese parents, they weren't exactly the hugging type. "I love you" wasn't something they said out loud. But every dish they prepared was a quiet declaration of love. I felt it in every bite.

I, on the other hand, have grown up more American—so I smother my own kids with hugs and kisses and tell them "I love you" every single day. But it also brings me immense joy to share my love through cooking. The dishes my parents once made for my brothers and me are now the ones my own children ask for and that I prepare for them with the same heart. From the very beginning, making sure our family was well-fed was an unshakable part of my identity—even if I didn't always serve five courses a night!

I'm proud to be an Asian American woman who's carved a path in an industry that too often overlooks stories like mine. But I know there's a hungry audience out there—hungry for flavor, hungry for culture, hungry for heart. For me, there's always been this lingering thought in the back of my mind: I wanted to write a cookbook as a tribute to my parents and to the restaurant. Not just because they gave us a good life—the classic American Dream—but because the restaurant was a source of so much more. It provided for us, yes, but it also gave something meaningful to Pittsburgh and to all our patrons. It became our community. It was how we gave back. The ripple effect of that—spreading love and culture through food—is something I deeply cherish. That idea stayed with me for a long time. And, in the end, it was the fans who became the spark to finally make this cookbook happen. You asked for it, and now I'm serving!

But first, let me take you back to where it all began.

My parents and older brother, Jun, found a way to leave China and start a new life in Macau, which was a Portuguese colony at the time and where I was born. My father worked odd jobs, and although my mother was a trained nurse, she couldn't practice in Macau because her credentials didn't transfer, so she worked as a caretaker of a kind, elderly man. He provided my parents with housing. When my mother became pregnant with me, my father decided to travel to Hong Kong in search of better work opportunities. My earliest memory is of taking possibly my first steps, walking toward the elderly man my mother cared for. He loved me, she says, and it gave him a lot of renewed energy to have a child in the house. I was around three when we left for Hong Kong to join my father. My mother remembers it was a sad day for everyone when we left, especially for her patient. I don't recall my parents divorcing, but apparently it happened soon after we moved to Hong Kong. My father faded into memory. My mother was suddenly raising Jun and me alone, juggling three jobs to make ends meet and put food on the table. Her nursing credentials didn't apply here, either, so by day, she again looked after elderly clients and picked up freelance jobs. By night, she sat in her armchair, brow furrowed under a single lamp, hand-beading dresses for a local tailor. The painstaking work strained her eyes and stole her sleep. But she was a survivor and was determined to make things work for our little family of three.

Looking back, I know we didn't have much. When money was tight, Mom rented out two of our bedrooms, and the three of us shared the remaining one. During the rainy season, storms soaked the city until our apartment walls bubbled with tiny, quivering pockets of water. For fun, I used to poke at them, popping the bubbles and watching the water seep out. (Hey—there was no internet! A kid had to get creative.) But I never felt poor. Our cramped apartment felt like a palace, and despite working endlessly, Mom still found time to cook. She'd shop the vibrant Hong Kong markets for fresh produce and meat, then stretch every dollar into something soulful. She cooked the dishes her own mother had taught her in Suzhou, our ancestral home west of Shanghai.

1. Hamming it up in Macau with the elderly man who adored me like a granddaughter.
2. A rare baby photo of me with Jonathan and my mother in 1963.
3. This is a rare picture of my mom's parents and my uncles in Suzhou in 1935. My grandmother was pregnant with my mom here.
4. Baby Ming in a stroller!
5. I love my poodle outfit and that random little cat prop!

One of my childhood favorites was her luscious noodle soup with pickled cabbage and pork. And her dumplings! Mountains of them, frozen in batches for easy weeknight meals. Her specialties were juicy pork and shrimp dumplings. She'd soak finely chopped ginger in water for an hour, then squeeze the gingery liquid into the filling for an extra punch of flavor. (My mouth waters just thinking about it.) Even her vegetables were something special—like her fragrant bok choy or her scrambled eggs with jiu cai (Chinese chives). She'd joke that the chives acted like little brooms in our stomachs, sweeping out the bad. Poetic intestinal advice, right? But she must have been onto something—Mom is ninety years young and healthier than most forty-year-olds. (I still eat that dish religiously. I'm convinced it keeps me youthful. And, well . . . regular.)

She saved diligently, too. Once a week, she'd treat us to chou doufu—"stinky tofu." We lived on the seventh floor, and if our windows were open, we could smell the vendor coming before he even got to the building. That's how strong the aromatic stink from that fermented tofu was! She'd give my brother some coins, and he'd race downstairs to grab some before it sold out. Sure, it stunk to high heaven, but once you bit into that crispy skin and chewy center, the smell was forgiven. I equate it to durian fruit or stinky cheese. And during Chinese New Year? Bing tanghulu! Ruby-red candied hawthorn berries on skewers—our version of candied apples. I gnawed on them proudly, certain I was bringing our family good fortune with every sticky bite.

When I was around five, my mother met a man from America who would become my father—Soo Lim Yee. They met at a dinner party while he was visiting Hong Kong on a business trip. He was smitten. They began a long-distance relationship, writing flowery love letters to each other. Frankly, I can't picture my stepfather, a rather stoic man of few words, being such a romantic. I love knowing this side of him. They would meet up for dinners whenever he flew to Hong Kong. After a couple of years of courtship, he helped sponsor our move to the United States.

Here's another thing about Chinese parents: They don't explain much to their kids. One morning when I was about seven, my mother woke Jun and me up early and said we were going out. That was it. No details on where we were headed. Next thing I knew, we were getting onto an airplane. Never having been on a plane or visited the airport before, I thought, *Ohh, this is fun!* Soon after takeoff, my mother told me we were moving to America. "What? What's America?" I asked her. My young, little mind immediately thought of the only things I knew as foreign, which were the stories about Jesus and the three wise men from the Catholic school we'd attended. (Mom had enrolled us there because it was right across the street from our apartment in Hong Kong. And even though she was raising us Buddhist, as a busy working mother, she found that the convenience of the school's location outweighed any religious affiliation.) I have memories of those nuns being very strict and often disciplining me with a ruler. Yeah, the good old days! I remember the Bible stories as my only frame of reference for foreign lands. I thought we were going to live in the desert and ride camels. I was shocked my mother would bring us to such a horrible place, and I cried buckets. "I don't want to live in the desert!" I complained. I don't think my mother had any idea what I was talking about. Well, imagine my relief when I looked out the plane's window and saw the New York City skyline rather than sand dunes. I was happy America looked just like Hong Kong.

SOON AFTER TAKEOFF, MY MOTHER TOLD ME WE WERE MOVING TO AMERICA. "WHAT? WHAT'S AMERICA?"

Once we were there, life opened up in surprising ways. When we first arrived, we stayed in Brooklyn with my stepfather's friends. They owned a real Chinese laundromat, the kind where the clothes are carefully wrapped in brown paper, tied with string, and ticketed on the package. There were so many new sights and sounds that I was overwhelmed, but I adapted as quickly as I could. I cannot even imagine what my mother and older brother were going through, but I'm sure their adjustments were even more intense than my own. Once we moved into our own apartment at Crescent House in Astoria, Queens, I was thrust into my first day of elementary school, probably second grade. When the bell rang, all the kids stood up to recite the Pledge of Allegiance. I had no idea what was going on. Everyone had their hands on their hearts and was looking toward the flag and reciting robotically. I was told to stand up, so I did. I looked around and thought, *Who are these people? What is happening here?* I didn't know any English yet, and this was quite a first impression and a major culture shock.

What helped to ease me into America's way of life? Pizza. One of my favorite new foods was New York pizza. We'd never had cheese before, and, in fact, my mom still doesn't like cheese, with the exception of having it on a slice of New York pizza. Go figure. What is it about the magic of a good New York slice? It's a universal comfort food!

1.

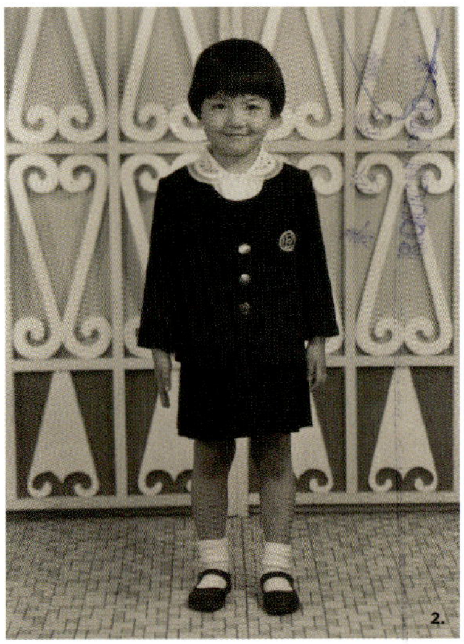

2.

3.

4.

1. This is my only picture of my whole family in front of the restaurant.
2. This looks like a school uniform to me, ready to go.
3. I love this shot of sassy me with a purse!
4. Did my mom give me a perm with this bowl cut?! Thanks a lot, Mom.

Luckily, having access to good Chinese food wasn't difficult. You just had to hop on the 4, 5, 6, or N train to get to Chinatown, where you could have a really decent meal. Thank goodness we didn't end up living in the desert, where I'll bet there was no dim sum. All of us felt we were adjusting to our new life whenever we ate at one of the many great Chinese restaurants New York City had to offer. And that's the beautiful thing about food, right? It helps you to feel at home no matter where you are. There are Chinatowns throughout the world. I know that there's a lot of talk about saving Chinatowns, as they are being encroached upon. They really are an important part of our history and worth saving, so if you live near a Chinatown, visit its restaurants and shops—you'll be helping to preserve an important part of Chinese culture.

Soon after we arrived in New York, my mother became pregnant with my younger brother, Lang. I was eight and remember the excitement of meeting him when my parents brought him home. He was the cutest little baby! We stayed in Astoria for about three years before moving to Pittsburgh to be with my stepfather and join him in running his restaurant, the Chinatown Inn. Growing up, I'd only known my own father first as a visitor, then just as a distant memory. With my stepfather becoming a consistent parent in my life, he easily became Baba ("Dad" in Chinese) to me.

At first we lived above the restaurant, and then my parents bought a small house in Mount Lebanon, where I enrolled at Jefferson Junior High School for sixth grade. Oh, boy, was that a tough transition! I went from a big city where I had friends, an urban lifestyle, and the diversity of New York to . . . well, white suburbia. I imported all my New York attitude and energy in my 4'11" body. Being one of, if not the only, Asian people at that school with a very Chinese name, I attracted some unfriendly sorts who made fun of me for how I looked or what my name sounded like. I was bullied. But I was a tough New Yorker, so I responded with a threat: "You want to settle this? I'll meet you after school!" Those innocent, sheltered suburban kids would give me a confused look and ask, "What do you mean? Meet you where?" I'm sure I wasn't very intimidating with my baby face and small self, but no one met me after school, either. (Perhaps that was my first inspiration for Mulan, Agent May, and all the other tough warrior-woman roles I would go on to portray in my acting career!) But we eventually settled into our life in Pittsburgh—my mother started to work in the restaurant, and the Chinatown Inn became a second home to me, as well as my part-time job. That place shaped my youth.

Even now, I can close my eyes and return to the bustle of that kitchen—the controlled chaos, the clatter of dishes, the constant hum of diners. The red-and-green pagoda entrance. The blinking neon sign. The clang of the cash register. The bustling bar. The pristine white tablecloths, which were always stained with a bit of soy sauce or stray grains of rice before they were swapped out for fresh ones. And always, at the end of the meal, a fortune cookie. The quintessential symbol of the Chinese American restaurant experience. American diners mostly ordered the classics: chow mein, fried rice, General Tso's chicken, shrimp with lobster sauce, our massive (not skimpy!) egg rolls. And our famous wonton soup. We made the stock fresh every morning using high-quality chicken and neck bones, simmering everything into a rich, amber broth. My dad always said that good ingredients make good food—and good food keeps the customers coming back, which is why I believe the Chinatown Inn is the only remaining business from the original Chinatown in downtown Pittsburgh. Our success story and longevity started with the basics. I've found that to be true in life, too—what you put in is what you get out.

Between the lunch and dinner rushes, our staff—bartenders, servers, cooks, my parents and siblings, and me—would gather for a family meal, sitting together and eating what we'd consider more traditional Chinese dishes. Stuff that was not on the menu but that you'll find in my cookbook. Dishes like steamed fish with ginger and scallions or black mushrooms and tofu. Many restaurants don't feed their employees, but my parents believed that doing otherwise was simply wrong. We shared stories, laughter, and food, then jumped back into service. Jun and I often did our homework in one of the back booths. Afterward, we filled saltshakers, took takeout orders, helped make wontons, or cleaned up. Then we did it all again the next day.

When we lived in Mount Lebanon, my dad would cook at home after working all day—he loved cooking for us, and Mom was always his sous chef. Cooking together was both a hobby and a passion that they loved sharing. And at every meal, there was soup. Always. That soup came to mind whenever I was chowing down on my starving-actor ramen soup in New York while trying to start my career.

The first time that I became interested in acting was in the third grade while we were still in New York. I was one of the bunny rabbits in an Easter play. My English was still a work in progress, and being a bunny rabbit (I played "Stumpy") meant I probably had the fewest lines.

I remember coming on stage and tripping because I had big bunny feet, and people laughed. Instead of being embarrassed, I loved the reaction that I got, and I thought, *I want to do this forever!* The acting bug bit me. Believe it or not, to this day I'm still clumsy. It's ironic that I do all these amazing martial arts and fight scenes on film and television; the Easter play audience that laughed at me had no idea they were witnessing a future action heroine!

As I grew up in Pittsburgh, the theater became a safe haven for me—I got to be with people of like minds, who were just the funniest, most intelligent, creative, and passionate people. Sometimes theater kids are shy. It's a weird combination, but in acting, you get to confidently transform into somebody else—it's just the purest form of escapism. We had a great training program at Mount Lebanon High School, and to this day, it's still incredible. I loved learning how to apply stage makeup, create characters, make costumes, and build sets, cooking up all those ingredients that bring a production together and make magic for the audience. Those were skills that I loved just as much as acting. It was a good base of knowledge for life in general. All the set building has helped me to become *very* good at putting furniture together. I also love figuring out ways to fix things with stuff we have around the house. I call it Ming-yvering, a fun take on the show *MacGyver*, if you will. I also love interior design, which is the profession I would have chosen if I hadn't become an actress.

WE SHARED STORIES, LAUGHTER, AND FOOD, THEN JUMPED BACK INTO SERVICE.

During my senior year of high school, I applied to Carnegie Mellon University because it had a great drama program and was in Pittsburgh, which made things easier. I knew I would go to New York City for the theater scene after college, so I figured this was a way I could spend four more years near my parents before pursuing my dreams to make it on Broadway. I had great grades and a high SAT score, so, at the time, I thought, *I'm getting into this college. There's no way I won't get into this college.* I didn't know I actually had to audition to be accepted into the drama program. I went into the audition thinking they just wanted to see where my skill levels were. I did my monologues. I did improv scenes. I was having a great time! I found out later that all my classmates were terribly nervous during the audition process. It wasn't until I got an acceptance letter saying "Congratulations. We loved your audition. We've accepted you into the freshman program" that it hit me. I didn't apply to any other colleges, so it was a good thing that I did well enough to be accepted! Perhaps it was because I was so relaxed. As they say, ignorance is bliss.

While at Carnegie Mellon, I still worked at the restaurant. I waitressed, hosted, ran the register, and even bartended. I ate many of my meals there because, well, it was free! But all along I knew that my destiny was to leave Pittsburgh after college. I saved every penny I made, and after I graduated, I hitched a U-Haul behind my parents' huge Cadillac and drove eight hours by myself to New York—with no GPS, mind you, just some maps from AAA guiding me. I think back on how worried my parents must've been for me. How did we do anything without cell phones back then?! A friend of my mother's had a tiny basement apartment in Elmhurst, Queens, so I took it sight unseen. I got there, unloaded, and, once I was settled into my new independent life, I just bawled. It was scary being on my own for the first time. At first, I had to use a pay phone to call my mom because my landline wasn't hooked up yet. I'm pretty sure I called collect because long-distance calls were expensive back then! I drove the Cadillac back to Pittsburgh and knew I was saying goodbye to the city forever. And I was right. All these decades later, I still haven't gone back to live there. Visit, yes. But somehow, even to this day, I always feel I'm a New Yorker at heart. That city made me who I am today. And now I was returning to conquer it.

I was chasing my acting dream, but it wasn't long before I missed home. I missed my parents. I missed their food. I did my best to cook from memory, but I was on a very tight budget, so most of the time I would grab three-dollar lunches from hot dog carts or get a sandwich or a dollar slice. Like many shoestring-budget kids who came before me, I made a lot of ramen in those days. Instant noodles and eggs, and I was good to go. It wasn't until later that I started to really learn to cook for myself, whipping up feasts in my tiny studio kitchen, impressing my parents when they came to visit. When you have two chefs in the family, they do all the cooking. You watch, you set the table, you do the dishes *a lot*. I don't think my parents ever asked my brother or me to help prep meals because the two of them were so efficient. But I was a restaurant daughter at heart—I had the palate, I knew the way things should taste, and I'd seen everything done a hundred times. A few years into living on my own in New York, I got good at cooking. Like, *really* good.

My big break in acting came in 1988, when I got a regular role on the steamy soap *As the World Turns*. I was doing a lot of off-Broadway

1.

2.

3.

4.

5.

1. October 30, 1992, was a very special day for me. This was the first table read of *The Joy Luck Club* with the full cast, which included Rosalind Chao, Lauren Tom, Tsai Chin, Kieu Chinh, me, Lisa Lu, France Nuyen, and Tamlyn Tomita, along with Janet Yang (producer), Amy Tan (author), Ron Bass (screenwriter), Wayne Wang (director), and crew members. It was my first time surrounded by Asian American talents, and my first time on a film project and getting to work with my idol, Amy Tan, on a book that changed my life and perspective on being Chinese American. Little did I know that this was the beginning of my career in Hollywood and my future role as wife and mother. It was because of *The Joy Luck Club* that I got to meet my husband, Eric Michael Zee.
2. The Disney Legends award was established in 1987. Since then, only 318 awards have been given, making this an incredible honor. You can see my handprints at the Disney Legends Plaza situated in front of the Team Disney building at Walt Disney Studios in Burbank, California.
3. I received Hollywood Star #2757 on May 30, 2023. It was truly an American Dream moment. My mother and Jonathan both cried, as this was a remarkable occasion for an immigrant from China.
4. Me with my with husband, Eric, and kids, Michaela and Cooper, at home in LA.
5. Serving dinner and eating together is one of my favorite family activites.

theater and working with companies like Manhattan Theatre Club, The Public Theater, and Playwrights Horizons. Getting the role of Lien Hughes, the first contracted role for an Asian American actor on the soap, was exciting. It was also the most I'd ever been paid for an acting gig! Since CMU didn't have a program to teach you how to perform in front of a camera, this was an intense master class in acting with cameras around. So many wonderful actors came out of that soap: Julianne Moore, Meg Ryan, and Marisa Tomei, to name a few. I then got a national commercial for Uncle Ben's Rice—I was Suzi Wan (food again!). I was flown out to LA to shoot it, my first taste of Hollywood. In 1993, the biggie came in the form of *The Joy Luck Club*, which was my first foray into the cinematic world. Reading Amy Tan's novel of the same name was life-altering for me. It was the first time I felt like I wasn't alone in my Asian American experience. I remember thinking after finishing the book that if it was ever made into a film, I wanted to be a part of it. I didn't care if I was acting in it or was a production assistant bringing people coffee—I just had to be involved in the project. How crazy that a few years later, I won the role of June, one of the main daughters in the book. I also became friends with Amy Tan and made lifelong friends with the other actresses in the film.

IN 1993, THE BIGGIE CAME IN THE FORM OF *THE JOY LUCK CLUB*, WHICH WAS MY FIRST FORAY INTO THE CINEMATIC WORLD.

I always joke that *The Joy Luck Club* was my green card to Hollywood. Over the decades, it has become such an iconic movie, particularly for Asian Americans, a poignant moment of feeling seen for so many. Journalist Lisa Ling once told me that fans often remember all the details of where they were and who they were with when they first saw it. How special to be part of a project that has had such a profound impact on someone's life. Another thing that Amy gets right is how food plays an additional character in *The Joy Luck Club*. The movie opens with a party scene showcasing platters of food. There is a heartbreaking scene of a mother feeding her daughter as a young child, only to have to give her away to another family; there's a funny scene in which Waverly's boyfriend pours soy sauce on a fish dish, which is an insult to her mom's cooking; and there's the infamous crab dinner scene where June later discovers from her mother that while Waverly might have taken the best-quality crab, she's proud of June for having the best-quality heart. Featuring food in the film emphasizes how gathering around a meal is such an integral part of our culture. It's how we show our love, sharing memories through tears and laughter.

I attribute meeting my husband, Eric Michael Zee, to *The Joy Luck Club*. (The juicy details can be found in the recipe for the Dragon Fruit Cheesecake Cups on page 233). Even though he was very attractive and we hit it off right away, it was because of food that he truly won my heart. He cooked and packed a picnic basket for our first date. We just celebrated our thirtieth anniversary on June 16, 2025, in Maui, where we eloped. We raised two incredible kids, Michaela and Cooper, and one of our proudest achievements is making sure they are foodies! I remember visiting Paris with them and eating at a local restaurant that was serving escargot. While another American family with their kids were eating hamburgers and "French" fries, our kids were trying escargot for the first time. They loved it so much, we ordered more. The parents next to us were so surprised our kids were willing to try eating snails. That was a very proud moment for us. Our adventures in all our travels include enjoying the local cuisines. That's the whole point of traveling! I truly believe the secret to my lasting marriage to Eric is because we are both passionate about food. We both can cook, and we love going out to eat. Many of the recipes in my cookbook share some favorite dishes from our family trips. Unfortunately, it does not include escargot. Maybe the next one!

Decades have passed, but the lessons from my parents' restaurant—and their recipes—are still with me. Food is family. It's how we survive, how we connect, and how we love. Even today, as I mentioned earlier, the Chinatown Inn still stands. As the last remaining restaurant from Pittsburgh's original Chinatown, it continues to serve generations of hungry diners. My brother Jun (now Jonathan) and his wife, Wei, own and run the restaurant now.

I've taken the flavors and values I grew up with into every role—whether as an actress, a wife, or a mom. I wrote *Have You Eaten Yet?* for all the home cooks who want to create love, memories, and connection through food. For fans who've followed me—from *ER* to *The Joy Luck Club*, from *Mulan* to *Agents of S.H.I.E.L.D.*, *The Mandalorian*, and beyond—I hope this is another meaningful way to connect.

My journey to America has been full of unexpected turns. You never really know where life will take you. For the longest time, I thought I wanted nothing to do with the restaurant business. I had seen the long

1.

2.

3.

4.

5.

1. This was the first time I saw a building-size wallscape of my film on Sunset Boulevard. A dream come true!
2. Pittsburgh pride! I chose "86" as my jersey number for the year I graduated from Carnegie-Mellon University. I really got into the Terrible Towel twirling, eh?
3. *Street Fighter* was my first foray into being a badass action hero. The OG Chun-Li.
4. Why, hello there, Agent May!
5. Being such a massive *Star Wars* fan, I totally geeked out when I saw myself featured on this *Book of Boba Fett* billboard.

hours my parents put in, and I'd worked countless hours there myself. That was exactly why I thought I'd go in a different direction.

And yet, here I am. As I've grown older, I've come to revere that experience. I now see what a gift it was to grow up in the restaurant—to be a restaurant daughter. It's one of those quiet realizations that grows stronger with time. The restaurant wasn't just a gift to us but to Pittsburgh as well. There's something so beautiful about a long-standing, family-owned place. It crosses generations. It becomes a marker of time, of tradition, and of the creation of new traditions. We were able to help shape those moments for people—to introduce them to new foods, new flavors—and become part of their stories, too.

So, let's cook together. Let's laugh and remember and celebrate. Because even if our backgrounds differ wildly, food is our universal language. And it all begins with a little love—and maybe a bit of ginger. Have *you* eaten yet?

HONG KONG WITH MOM

These are the dishes of my childhood—the ones I remember from growing up in bustling, fast-paced Hong Kong.

My mother (Wang Lin Chan) and older brother, Jun (aka Jonathan), and I lived in a crowded three-bedroom apartment. To make ends meet, my mother rented out two of the bedrooms to a married couple and one older gentleman. Even though she juggled several jobs as a single mom, she still found the time and energy to make magic in our small kitchen, not just for us but also for her tenants. Some of the recipes she brought with her from her hometown of Suzhou—simple, soulful food that tasted like home—and she picked up others along the way, learning to cook local Hong Kong favorites. She even bartered with her cooking. For example, when she had to work late, she would cook dried tofu and Chinese celery (the older man's favorite dish) in exchange for his watching my brother and me at night.

Looking back now, as a mom myself, I have a whole new appreciation for how much she carried. Life in Hong Kong wasn't easy, but she never made it seem that way. She worked hard, cooked harder, and never let us feel like we were missing a thing. When I'd ask how she did it all, she'd shrug and say, "When I was young, I felt invincible, like I could do anything." And you know what? She did. And so much more. She is a warrior woman who made many sacrifices for us. Her intelligence, resilience, and

2.

3.

4.

5.

6.

7.

8.

1. (previous page) Mom, baby Ming-na, and Jonathan in Macau.
2. On a stroll in a park in Macau with my mom.
3. Me, my mom, and Jonathan on a street in either Hong Kong or Macau. This was her dressing "casually" for an outing. A far cry from my own sweats and ponytail look! She was so stylish.
4. Me posing in front of a palm tree.
5. Oh, I used to love this baby doll!
6. Cute overalls, but why do you keep perming my hair, Mom?
7. Me with my supermodel mom!
8. My mother and me in Macau, demurely showing some leg.

survival skills inspire me every day. I don't doubt that I got the part of Mulan, the young female warrior, because of her influence.

This chapter is for her—the flavors, the memories, and the quiet strength behind every dish. From crispy pork chops to mapo tofu, from curry chicken to sweet-and-sour fish—these recipes are more than food. Over the years, my husband and our two children have also shared many wonderful meals with my mom. My children call her Popo, and they grew up with her cooking, as I did. Food is a marker for the love, laughter, and traditions we get to share as a family. I want to bring a little taste of our home to you.

1.

2.

3.

4.

5.

1. Here with Mom, my first stylist.
2. My brothers, Mom, and me in front of the restaurant.
3. My mother and me in front of the ruins of St. Paul's Cathedral in Macau.
4. My brother was photobombing me here, clearly!
5. This is when we went back to Hong Kong with my mom. I wanted to see where I grew up, and this is the apartment building. It says Incorporated Owners of National Court; I don't know what that indicates—perhaps it was government subsidized—but this brought back some of my oldest memories!

POPO'S WONTONS

PREP TIME: 45 MINUTES, PLUS 30 MINUTES MARINATING TIME

COOK TIME: 15 MINUTES

MAKES ABOUT 60 WONTONS

Wontons hold a special place in my heart. Sitting around our kitchen table making wontons is something I loved doing with my mother as a child. Time was scarce, so the chance to make wontons with her became special mother-daughter moments for us. She always had all the fillings ready to go—my favorite was and still is pork, shrimp, and vegetables. I'd carefully scoop a bit of filling onto the wonton wrapper and do my best to fold it as neatly as possible. Years later, I've continued the tradition with my own children, and together as a family we make Popo's wontons ("Popo" is the Chinese word for "maternal grandmother"). Just as it was for my mother and me, making wontons gives me and my kids the opportunity to escape the chaos of daily life and bond while we fold together. It also gives me the chance to share more about our heritage. For example, the Chinese revere wealth (like most people!), and wontons are a symbol for gold—when folding, your goal is to create a wonton shaped like a Chinese gold ingot. (I suppose that's one way of getting rich.) My kids thought it was the silliest, most fun thing to eat "gold."

1 (3-inch) knob peeled ginger, minced

½ pound large (31/40) raw shrimp, shelled and deveined

2 tablespoons cornstarch, divided

2 teaspoons kosher salt, divided

1 pound frozen shepherd's purse, defrosted (or 2 bunches fresh watercress)

2 tablespoons light soy sauce

1 tablespoon vegetable oil

½ teaspoon ground white pepper

1 pound ground meat (pork, turkey, or chicken)

1 large egg

2 (12-ounce) packages square, thin wonton wrappers (you won't use them all)

1 • In a small bowl, soak the ginger in ¼ cup of water for 15 minutes.

2 • Rinse the shrimp with cold water. Drain them and place in a medium bowl with 1 tablespoon of the cornstarch, massaging it gently into the shrimp to further clean them. Rinse the shrimp again with clean, cold water. Drain them, then toss with ½ teaspoon of the salt. Finely chop the shrimp. Set aside.

3 • Rinse the defrosted shepherd's purse with cold water, then squeeze out the excess water. Finely chop the greens, then toss them with ½ teaspoon of the salt. Set aside. (If using watercress, boil 2 bunches for 3 minutes, then drain and rinse with cold water. Squeeze out the excess water and finely chop.)

(RECIPE CONTINUES)

4 • Remove the ginger from the water and squeeze it over the water to retain as much of the ginger-scented soaking water as possible. Discard the ginger, keeping only the ginger water.

5 • In a medium nonreactive bowl, combine the ginger water, soy sauce, the remaining 1 teaspoon of salt, oil, the remaining 1 tablespoon of cornstarch, and the white pepper. Add the ground meat and thoroughly mix it with the seasoning. Add the shrimp and greens and mix everything together. Allow it to marinate, covered in the refrigerator, for 30 minutes. Take a small piece and cook the meat mixture in boiling water until the meat floats, about 3 minutes. Taste it to see if it's seasoned well. If not, add another teaspoon of salt to the meat and mix well.

6 • In a small bowl, whisk the egg so that it can be used to seal the wonton skins.

7 • Fan the stack of skins out to create a pinwheel of skins. This separates the skins, making them easier to pick up. Take one wonton skin and place a dollop of meat mixture (about ½ tablespoon) in the center.

8 • Using the tip of a butter knife dipped in the egg, brush the top and side edges of the skin. Fold the square in half and gently press the edges together. The wonton is now a rectangle. Brush the bottom corners with egg. Holding the rectangle in your palm, bend the left and right corners together toward the center of the wonton. Squeeze the corners together to seal.

9 • On a tray or plate lined with parchment paper, place the wontons in rows with a bit of separation between them so that they do not stick together. Make sure the tray or plate will fit in your freezer. Once the tray is full, freeze the wontons until the skin feels solid and frozen, about 1 hour. You can then place the wontons in a plastic freezer bag without worrying about them sticking together. Immediately place the bag back in the freezer to further freeze the wontons. Remember to write a date on the bags. They will keep for 3 to 4 months.

10 • If you're starting with fresh wontons, bring a large pot of water to a boil. Leave enough room in the pot for 1 to 2 cups of additional water. Add the wontons. When the water boils again, add ½ cup cold water. When the water boils again, add another ½ cup of cold water. When the wontons float to the top, they are done. Adding cold water in steps like this keeps the skin of the wontons from overcooking and becoming too soft.

11 • With frozen wontons, repeat the above, but add ½ cup cold water one more time because the frozen meat needs a bit longer to cook through.

COOK'S NOTE: *Serve the wontons with whatever sauce you like, such as a chili sauce, soy sauce with Chinkiang vinegar, or just soy sauce. You can also serve as a wonton soup with chicken broth and vegetables and noodles (recipe follows).*

Wonton Soup Broth

SERVED WITH THE WONTONS
SERVES: 4

- 4 (1-inch) bundles dry Chinese egg noodles or fine Japanese noodles (optional)
- 4 cups chicken stock, homemade if possible
- 4 to 6 bok choy heads, chopped, or 2 cups chopped napa cabbage
- 1 tablespoon light soy sauce
- 1 teaspoon kosher salt, divided, plus more for seasoning
- ½ teaspoon ground white pepper, divided, plus more for seasoning
- 16 to 24 freshly boiled wontons (recipe above)
- 2 scallions, white and green parts, chopped
- 1 teaspoon sesame oil (optional)
- 1 teaspoon chili sauce (optional)

1 • If desired, bring a large pot of water to a boil and boil the noodles, following the instructions on the package, minus 1 minute. Remove the noodles and rinse them under cold water to stop the cooking, then set aside.

2 • In a large pot over high heat, bring the chicken stock to a boil. Add the bok choy or cabbage, 1 cup of water, the soy sauce, and the salt and pepper. Simmer until the bok choy or cabbage is tender, about 5 minutes.

3 • Make individual bowls of wonton noodle soup by adding 4 to 6 wontons, some noodles (if using), broth, and bok choy. Sprinkle the soup with the chopped scallions and season with sesame oil, chili sauce, and more salt and white pepper, if desired.

PREP TIME: 20 MINUTES

COOK TIME: 18 MINUTES

SERVES: 4

SWEET-AND-SOUR MANDARIN FISH

3 tilapia, cod, or Chilean sea bass fillets (about 1 pound total)

Large bowl of ice water

FOR THE SWEET-AND-SOUR SAUCE

2 tablespoons vegetable oil, divided

½ white onion, cut into 1-inch chunks

2 scallions, white and green parts, cut in 2-inch strips

½ cup ketchup

½ tablespoon Shaoxing Chinese cooking wine

¼ cup granulated sugar

2 tablespoons honey

¼ cup white vinegar

2 tablespoons cornstarch mixed with 1 tablespoon water

At restaurants, this dish is usually beautifully presented as a whole-fish centerpiece, often eliciting "oohs" and "aahs" along with applause from the table when it's served. As with my steamed fish, I have adapted this for home and use fillets so you can easily make it whenever you want. You'll find it's just as yummy even if it's not as grandstanding. Though, hey, why not request a round of applause anyway? You got a delicious dinner on the table—you deserve it.

1 • First, make sure the fillets are defrosted and rinsed with cold water. Pat them dry with paper towels. Score the fillets by cutting ½-inch slits two-thirds of the way into the flesh, being careful not to go completely through the fillets. Then turn the knife to create a grid pattern or crisscross cuts. Dunk the fillets in the bowl of ice water. Set aside.

2 • MAKE THE SWEET-AND-SOUR SAUCE: Heat a medium saucepan or wok over medium-high heat and add 1 tablespoon of the vegetable oil. Add the onion and scallions and cook, stirring constantly, to bring out the aromatics, about 2 minutes. Add the ketchup, splash the edge of the wok with the cooking wine, then add the sugar and honey and stir everything together for 30 seconds. Add ⅔ cup water and the vinegar and stir until the sauce appears glassy, about 30 seconds. Then add the cornstarch slurry to thicken the sauce. Remove from the heat and pour the mixture into another saucepan. Remove and discard the scallions and onions to avoid flavoring the sweet-and-sour sauce any further. Set aside.

3 • MAKE THE FILLETS: Remove the fish fillets from the water bath and pat them dry as much as possible with paper towels. In a shallow, wide bowl, whisk the egg. In another shallow, wide bowl, mix together the cornstarch, salt, and pepper. Dip the fillets in the egg, then dredge them thoroughly in the seasoned cornstarch, coating all the crevices.

(RECIPE & INGREDIENTS CONTINUE)

FOR THE FILLETS:

1 large egg

1 cup cornstarch, or enough to cover all fillets

1 teaspoon kosher salt

½ teaspoon ground white pepper

3 cups vegetable, corn, or peanut oil for deep-frying

¼ cup frozen peas, defrosted (optional)

1 tablespoon almond slivers (optional)

4 • Heat a wok over medium-high heat, then add enough oil to deep-fry the fillets. Heat the oil to 300°F and fry one fillet at a time. If you do not have a thermometer, then watch the oil heat until it slightly bubbles on the side of the wok or some steam is seen. Cook the fillet to a light golden color, 3 or 4 minutes, then remove it using a large metal ladle with holes. Drain off the oil, then set the fish on paper towels to absorb any excess oil. Continue to deep-fry until all the fillets are cooked to a light golden color.

5 • Increase the heat of the oil to 350°F and refry the fillets until they reach a deeper golden color, 30 to 60 seconds. Again, remove them from the oil and drain in a ladle with holes over a pot or on paper towels.

6 • Reheat the sweet-and-sour sauce in a saucepan over medium heat, and add some cooked peas for color, if desired. Pour the sauce over the fried fillets on a platter and serve immediately. You can also garnish with almond slivers, if desired.

SCALLION PANCAKES

PREP TIME: 20 MINUTES PLUS 30 MINUTES FOR RISING

COOK TIME: 40 MINUTES

SERVES: 8

I always loved my mother's scallion pancakes but never thought to ask her to teach me to make them, probably because I always thought she was too busy. But I remember when I was around eleven years old, I finally asked, and she gave me her precious time—and probably a lot of patience—to show me how to make them. This moment stands out for me because it was rare for my mom to have time to teach me in the restaurant kitchen.

Back then, she always used lard to grease up the pancakes. These days, I use vegetable or avocado oil. I freeze any leftovers by putting parchment paper between each uncooked pancake and stacking two or three in a resealable plastic bag or tinfoil. When you're ready to cook them, just take them out, defrost for 15 minutes, and pan-fry them.

FOR THE DOUGH:

1 (17.6-ounce) bag or 4 cups fortified bread flour

1 cup hot water, divided

1 cup warm water, divided

FOR THE PASTE:

⅔ cup vegetable oil

½ cup all-purpose flour

¼ teaspoon ground white pepper

¼ teaspoon freshly ground black pepper

Kosher salt

8 scallions, white and green parts, chopped

3 tablespoons vegetable oil, divided, plus more for prepping rolling pin

FOR THE DIPPING SAUCE:

¼ cup Chinkiang vinegar

1 tablespoon plus 1 teaspoon soy sauce

1 tablespoon plus 1 teaspoon hot sauce

1 • MAKE THE DOUGH: Scoop the flour into a large mixing bowl. Gradually add ¼ cup of hot water at a time, mixing using a pair of chopsticks or a spatula to start forming the dough. Then do the same with the warm water. The dough will be very sticky and soft. Thoroughly mix the dough by hand at this point. (You can also use an electric mixer to make the dough, using the dough attachment.) Set the dough aside for 30 to 45 minutes to allow it to rise.

2 • On a well-floured surface or silicone mat to prevent it from sticking, roll the dough out into a long narrow log, then cut it in half. Then roll each of the halves out again into logs and cut them each into 4 equal pieces. Roll each piece into a round bun, for a total of 8.

3 • MAKE THE PASTE: Warm the oil in a small saucepan over medium-high heat until it ripples on top, but not to the point of smoking, then add the flour to the hot oil and mix well. Mix in the white and black pepper, then remove it from the heat.

(RECIPE CONTINUES)

4 • Prep the rolling pin by smearing the whole pin with vegetable oil. Take one of the dough balls and roll it out into a thin round pancake, about 12 inches in diameter. The dough will want to shrink back as you stretch it out. Make sure there are no tears. Smear a thin layer of paste over the entire pancake. Season the pancake with 4 to 5 pinches of salt and sprinkle it with a handful of scallions.

5 • Take the dough end closest to you and fold it over about ¼ inch, then continue rolling up the entire pancake. Take one end of the cigar shape that you now have and coil it into a spiral until you reach the other end, making a cinnamon bun–type shape. Tuck loose ends underneath the bun and pinch to secure them.

6 • Take a 12-inch piece of plastic wrap and put it under the bun. Flatten the bun with the palm of your hand. Take another 12-inch piece of plastic wrap and place it on top of the flattened bun. With the rolling pin, flatten the entire bun into a 6 to 8-inch pancake. Repeat with the other pieces until you've made all 8 pancakes. They can be frozen at this point if you wrap the edges of the plastic wrap tightly around each pancake.

7 • To cook the pancakes, heat a large sauté pan over medium-high heat, heat 1 teaspoon of the oil, then brown the pancakes for 3 to 5 minutes on each side, lowering the heat to medium if they brown too quickly. Repeat with the remaining pancakes, adding oil as needed.

8 • MAKE THE DIPPING SAUCE: In a small bowl, combine the vinegar, soy sauce, and hot sauce.

9 • Scallion pancakes are good alone or sliced into wedges and served with the dipping sauce.

PREP TIME: 15 MINUTES

COOK TIME: 10 MINUTES

SERVES: 4 TO 5

CRISPY FIVE-SPICE PORK CHOPS

6 boneless pork loin chops (can substitute boneless chicken thighs)

½ teaspoon kosher salt, divided

½ teaspoon ground white pepper (black pepper works, too)

1 teaspoon five-spice powder

1 teaspoon light soy sauce mixed with 1 teaspoon water

5 garlic cloves, chopped

1 cup panko breadcrumbs

1 cup plain breadcrumbs

1 teaspoon garlic powder

2 large eggs

2 tablespoons water

1 cup corn or vegetable oil

Cooked white rice, for serving (see page 236)

When I was growing up, my mom would take my brother and me to New York City's Chinatown for dinner and order five-spice pork chops over noodle soup. It was my own personal holiday because Mom never made them at home, and they. Were. So. Good.

It was around 1998, when *Mulan* had just come out, and I was settling into life both in Hollywood and as a wife and new mom. We had our first house and our first baby, beautiful Michaela. My mom was visiting us and we were having a barbecue party for Michaela's first birthday. Out of nowhere, she decided to make these pork chops as the main attraction. When she started deep-frying them, the smell of the garlic and five-spice powder immediately made everyone's mouth water. When she served them, we couldn't get enough; they disappeared almost immediately. I have no idea where or when Mom learned the recipe, but it makes me smile knowing that she still has such a love for cooking and enjoys feeding everyone. I want you to find that joy, too!

1 • Slice the pork loins in half horizontally to make thinner pieces: Placing the palm of your hand flat on top of the meat, with the knife parallel to the cutting board, cut through the side of each loin to divide it in two. Using kitchen shears or a knife, make shallow snips or cuts in the edges going around the pork loin chops, in several places, to prevent them from curling up when frying. Trim the fat, if desired.

2 • Put the pork loins into a plastic bag and pound to flatten them slightly to about ⅓ inch thick. I usually place a towel under the chopping board to prevent it from moving and to protect the countertop from the pounding. Remove the loins and lightly sprinkle both sides with the salt and white pepper.

(RECIPE CONTINUES)

3 • In a large mixing bowl, add one slice of pork loin, sprinkle some of the the five-spice powder and soy sauce over the top, then layer the second pork loin slice on top and repeat for all the slices.

4 • Put the chopped garlic in a large resealable plastic bag and add the seasoned chops. Allow them to marinate with the garlic for 10 to 15 minutes.

5 • In a shallow dish or plate, combine the panko, plain breadcrumbs, garlic powder, and a pinch of salt. In another shallow bowl, whisk the eggs and water together.

6 • Dip the marinated pork loins into the egg mixture on both sides. Let the excess drip off before putting the loins into the bowl with the breadcrumb mixture, then coat the chops completely in the mixture and put them on a clean plate.

7 • Heat the oil in a large wok or deep skillet over medium-high heat. Place the meat in the wok and deep-fry until golden brown, 3 to 4 minutes on each side. Transfer the cooked chops to a paper towel-lined cutting board to absorb the excess oil. Let the chops rest for 5 minutes.

8 • Serve the chops whole or sliced into pieces, over rice.

PREP TIME: 20 MINUTES

COOK TIME: 10 MINUTES

SERVES: 3 TO 4

SPICY PORK
WITH HOT PEPPER AND BAMBOO SHOOTS

1 tablespoon light soy sauce

1 tablespoon cornstarch

2 tablespoons plus
4 teaspoons vegetable oil,
divided

½ tablespoon dark soy sauce

1 pound pork loin, sliced into
¼-inch strips (see Cook's Note)

4 serrano peppers
(adjust to heat preference)

2 Anaheim peppers

1 (14-ounce) can julienned
bamboo shoots,
drained and rinsed

1 teaspoon kosher salt

Cooked white rice, for serving
(see page 236)

Take what I say next very seriously, folks: If you don't cook this dish outside, everyone inside will be subject to coughing fits. Really. Now, I know most people don't have an outdoor kitchen, but you've been warned. Crack open a window, chefs! This is one of those dishes that wallops your taste buds and your senses. It's so worth it, though. I swear I can feel the neurons in my brain firing faster when I eat this.

The bamboo shoots and rice cut the heat from the peppers nicely, but you really have to know your heat tolerance and adjust as needed—think about starting with milder peppers. I can guarantee that you'll want it hotter the next time you make it, so increase the heat gradually. If you're still finding everything too spicy, try adjusting the ratio of serrano peppers to Anaheim peppers, or swap them out entirely—serranos are eight times hotter than Anaheims. See you outside!

1 • In a medium nonreactive bowl or dish, combine the light soy sauce, cornstarch, 2 teaspoons of the vegetable oil, and the dark soy sauce. Mix the pork loin into the marinade and set aside in the refrigerator for 15 to 20 minutes.

2 • Using latex gloves to prevent your fingers from touching the spicy serrano peppers' oil, cut the serrano and Anaheim peppers into thin strips.

3 • In a heated wok over medium-high heat, add 2 tablespoons of the oil and heat it until it shimmers. Add the pork loin strips and cook, stirring constantly, until seared, about 2 minutes on each side, then stir in the wok for 2 minutes more to ensure that the pork is cooked through. Remove and set aside on a plate.

(RECIPE CONTINUES)

4 • Add the remaining 2 teaspoons of oil to the wok, toss in the peppers, and cook, stirring until fragrant and tender, about 2 minutes. (You may start choking a bit from the pepper fumes!) Toss in the bamboo shoots and salt and cook, stirring, for another minute. Add the cooked pork and stir-fry until warmed through, about 1 minute. Add 1 to 2 tablespoons of water if it's too dry.

5 • Transfer to a plate and serve with a lot of rice.

COOK'S NOTE: *It's easier to cut the pork into strips if it's slightly frozen. Slice the pork loin into ¼-inch slices, then lay the pieces flat and cut them into strips.*

PREP TIME: 15 MINUTES

COOK TIME: 20 MINUTES

SERVES: 4

CHINESE FLAT CABBAGE AND PORK

2 teaspoons light soy sauce, divided

½ teaspoon dark mushroom soy sauce

2 tablespoons plus 2 teaspoons vegetable oil, divided

1 teaspoon cornstarch

8 ounces pork loin, sliced into ¼-inch strips (see Cook's Notes)

1 whole scallion, cut into thirds

1 (¼-inch) slice peeled ginger (about the diameter of a quarter)

1 head Chinese flat cabbage or white cabbage, hand-torn into 2-inch pieces (see Cook's Notes)

¾ cup chicken broth or water, divided

1 garlic clove, minced

1 teaspoon kosher salt

⅛ teaspoon ground white pepper

1 tablespoon cornstarch mixed with 1 tablespoon water

Cooked white rice, for serving (see page 236)

Chinese flat cabbage (aka Taiwanese cabbage) has a more disk-like shape, as well as a denser texture, than napa cabbage, but its leaves are not as dense and thick as American cabbage. When you cook it, a nice sweetness develops. I discovered it years ago when we were visiting China. I was not familiar with flat cabbage, so, at the restaurant, I ordered it on a whim and was stunned by how yummy it was! We loved it so much that we got two more orders for the table. What a discovery!

As simple as this dish is, the crunch and sweetness of the cabbage alongside the aromatic garlic is incredibly flavorful. Try it with meat, as I've done here, or without—it makes a great vegan dish, too.

1 • In a medium nonreactive bowl, combine 1 teaspoon of the soy sauce, the mushroom soy sauce, 2 teaspoons of the vegetable oil, and the cornstarch. Add the pork strips and mix well with the seasoning. Set aside.

2 • Heat the wok over medium-high heat and add 1 tablespoon of the oil. Add the scallion and ginger to flavor the oil, then add the seasoned pork strips. Allow the meat to sit for 1 minute to sear before turning it over and searing again for 1 minute, then cook, stirring constantly, until all sides are browned, about 1 minute more. Remove from the wok and set aside.

3 • Add the remaining tablespoon of the oil to the wok and toss in the cabbage. Cook, stirring constantly to prevent burning. Splash about half of the chicken broth into the wok. Add the remaining teaspoon of soy sauce, the garlic, salt, and white pepper and stir-fry until the cabbage is tender but still has crunch, about 5 minutes. Depending on the size of your cabbage head, you may need to add more salt.

(RECIPE CONTINUES)

4 • Toss the pork strips back into the wok and mix with the cabbage. Add the remaining broth. Make a well in the center and stir in the cornstarch slurry to slightly thicken the liquid.

5 • Transfer to a plate and serve with rice.

COOK'S NOTES: *It's easier to cut the pork into strips if it's slightly frozen. Slice the pork loin into ¼-inch slices, then lay the pieces flat and cut them into strips.*

If you can't find flat cabbage, sometimes referred to as Taiwanese cabbage, you can use white cabbage, but it won't have the same sweetness or delicate texture. A friend taught me to hand-tear the tender green parts of the leaves and to discard most of the white parts nearer to the core and stem. I can't say why, but I can attest that her method does make the cabbage taste better than if it were cut into pieces with a knife!

PREP TIME: 15 MINUTES

COOK TIME: 20 MINUTES

SERVES: 4

CHESTNUT CHICKEN

1 pound 5 ounces chicken party wings (usually 1 package)

1 teaspoon kosher salt, divided

½ teaspoon Shaoxing Chinese cooking wine

⅛ teaspoon ground white pepper

1 whole scallion

1 cup chicken broth

1 teaspoon dark mushroom soy sauce

½ teaspoon light soy sauce

½ teaspoon granulated sugar

1 tablespoon vegetable oil, divided

3 (¼-inch) slices peeled ginger (about the diameter of a quarter)

⅓ cup diced onions

1 (5.2-ounce) package shelled roasted chestnuts, ½ cut in half and the rest left whole

1 teaspoon cornstarch mixed with 2 teaspoons water

Cooked white rice, for serving (see page 236)

Before everything became available prepackaged, chestnuts were not as easy to come by, and it was difficult for my mother to roast and peel them. Because the chestnuts were such a pain in the you-know-what to prepare, this was always a rare, special dish that my brothers and I looked forward to. When we lived in Hong Kong, I loved to walk by the carts that sold roasted chestnuts on the streets—the sweet, nutty aroma was incredible. Imagine my delight as a kid to find that Manhattan also had these carts!

Of course, when you buy the already-packaged peeled and cooked chestnuts, they don't taste as good as the freshly roasted ones. There's just a deeper, more robust flavor when you roast fresh, and you get a nice drier texture, too. So, if you're able to track down uncooked chestnuts and you have some time on your hands, I highly recommend DIYing it. And if there are any leftovers, let the dish sit overnight—it'll be even more delicious because the flavors will have had time to meld.

1 • Rinse the chicken wings and pat dry. Slice off and discard the tips, cut through the joint at the drumette, then chop the drumette and the wing in two, through the bone, to make 4 pieces total per chicken wing. (It's always best to use a cleaver and place a towel or a corkboard under the chopping board to protect your counter and to prevent the chopping board from slipping.)

2 • In a nonreactive dish or bowl, combine ½ teaspoon of the salt, the cooking wine, and the white pepper. Add the chicken wings and toss to coat. Make sure everything is evenly distributed and place in the refrigerator to marinate for 15 minutes.

3 • Cut the scallion in half, julienne both the green and white sections separately, and set aside.

(RECIPE CONTINUES)

4 • In a medium bowl, add the chicken broth, mushroom soy sauce, light soy sauce, and sugar and stir to dissolve the sugar.

5 • In a large sauté pan over medium-high heat, heat ½ tablespoon of the vegetable oil. Add the white part of the scallion and the ginger and cook, stirring, for 30 seconds. Toss in the marinated chicken wings. Allow one side to brown, about 3 minutes, then turn the wings over to brown the other side.

6 • Add the diced onions and the remaining ½ tablespoon of vegetable oil and cook, stirring everything well, until the onions soften, 2 to 3 minutes. Add the chestnuts and continue to stir frequently for 2 minutes.

7 • Pour in the chicken broth mixture and turn the heat up to high to bring the liquid to a boil. Make sure the liquid covers most of the chicken and chestnuts. Turn the heat down and cover the pan. Simmer for 10 minutes.

8 • Remove the cover and add the remaining ½ teaspoon salt, or salt to taste. Turn the heat up to medium-high again and add the cornstarch slurry to thicken the broth. Stir constantly until the gravy becomes slightly glossy, then immediately turn off the heat.

9 • Transfer to a large bowl, garnish with green scallion slivers, and serve hot.

CANTONESE CURRY CHICKEN

PREP TIME: 15 MINUTES

COOK TIME: 30 MINUTES

SERVES: 4

FOR THE CHICKEN MARINADE:

1 tablespoon oyster sauce

½ tablespoon golden curry powder

½ tablespoon Shaoxing Chinese cooking wine

1 teaspoon chicken bouillon

1 teaspoon kosher salt

1½ pounds boneless skinless chicken thighs

2 tablespoons cornstarch, divided

FOR THE CURRY:

2 medium Idaho potatoes

2 medium carrots, peeled and chopped

4 tablespoons vegetable oil, divided

1 medium onion, diced

2 whole scallions, cut into thirds, plus 1 scallion chopped, for garnish

2 (¼-inch) slices of peeled ginger (about the diameter of a quarter)

3 garlic cloves, cut in half

Growing up, I always thought of curry as Chinese, only to learn that curry originated in India. It is derived from the Tamil word *kari*, meaning "sauce," which the Chinese called *gali*. I didn't even know about all the varieties of curries in the world until I started dabbling in Indian food when I moved to New York City after college. Despite my kitchen travels, this has always been the original curry for me, the one that my mother made. The brand of curry paste you use is key for good flavor, and S&B Golden Curry is worth hunting down, either at a grocery store or an Asian market. I don't add cauliflower here as my mother used to—but I do in my veggie curry (page 67). It's great comfort food in wintertime. Round it out by serving it with rice.

1 • MAKE THE MARINADE: In a small bowl, combine the oyster sauce, golden curry powder, cooking wine, bouillon, and salt.

2 • Fill a large bowl with fresh water and submerge the chicken thighs. Gently squeeze out the excess water. Discard the water and repeat the soaking with fresh water. Dry the chicken with some paper towels. Remove as much of the fat as you can and cut the thighs into 2-inch chunks. Add to a large bowl.

3 • Apply the marinade to the chicken, rubbing it evenly into all parts. Sprinkle the cornstarch, ½ tablespoon at a time, over the chicken, turning it to evenly cover all parts. Allow the chicken to marinate, covered in the refrigerator, for 15 minutes. (Always make sure to thoroughly wash your hands and any surfaces that come into contact with raw chicken.)

4 • MAKE THE CURRY: While the chicken is marinating, peel and cut the potatoes into 1½-inch cubes, then place in a bowl with water to cover. Drain the potatoes and dry them in a towel. If the carrots are still wet, dry them as well.

(RECIPE & INGREDIENTS CONTINUE)

5 • Heat a wok over high heat. Add ½ tablespoon of the oil. Once the oil is hot, add the onion and cook, stirring constantly, for 1 minute, then remove and set aside.

6 • Add another ½ tablespoon of the oil to the wok. Add the potatoes and cook, stirring constantly, for 2 minutes. Then add the carrots and continue to stir-fry for 2 minutes. Remove and set aside.

7 • Add 2 tablespoons of the oil to the wok over high heat. Add the scallions and ginger to flavor the oil, then add the marinated chicken. Allow it to brown on one side for 1 minute before flipping. Brown the second side for 1 minute, then continue to cook the chicken, stirring constantly, for 2 more minutes.

8 • Add the potatoes, carrots, garlic, wine, and remaining 1 tablespoon oil to the wok and stir-fry for 2 minutes. Add the hot water and broth, which should be just enough liquid to cover the chicken and vegetables.

9 • Bring the mixture to a boil, then cover and reduce the heat to a simmer for approximately 5 minutes. Add the onion, curry paste square, coconut milk, salt, golden curry powder, and sugar and simmer for 5 minutes.

10 • Test the potatoes to make sure they are done by piercing with a fork. They should be just cooked through but not overcooked. Add the white pepper and taste-test. Add more curry or salt to your preference. The consistency of the curry sauce should be like a smooth gravy, not too thick or too watery.

11 • Put everything into a large bowl, garnish with the chopped scallion, and serve with rice.

1 teaspoon Shaoxing Chinese cooking wine

2 cups hot water

1 cup hot chicken broth

1 square (about 2 tablespoons) S&B Golden Curry medium-spice bouillon paste

2 tablespoons canned whole-fat coconut milk

½ teaspoon kosher salt

½ teaspoon S&B Golden Curry powder

½ teaspoon granulated sugar

⅛ teaspoon ground white pepper

Cooked white rice, for serving (see page 236)

YU CHOY
WITH OYSTER SAUCE

PREP TIME: 10 MINUTES

COOK TIME: 10 MINUTES

SERVES: 4

1 pound yu choy

1 tablespoon vegetable oil

½ teaspoon kosher salt

2 tablespoons oyster sauce

¼ teaspoon ground white pepper

Yu choy is a leafy vegetable that is often referred to as Chinese broccoli. LOL. I find this amusing because lots of vegetables we use in our cooking end up being translated as "Chinese broccoli." Yu choy, however, looks nothing like broccoli, nor does it taste like it—I'd say it's closer in taste to bok choy or baby spinach. You can often find it served at dim sum as a vegetable dish. I like to serve it as a vegetable side, but sometimes, if I need a quick and healthy meal, I make yu choy and have it with some rice.

1 • Wash and drain the yu choy. Peel the stalks to remove any tough layers. Set aside.

2 • Bring a pot of water to a boil. Add the oil and salt to the water, then add the yu choy. Once the water boils again, cook for 2 minutes. Remove the greens with tongs, drain, and place on a serving plate.

3 • Drizzle the greens with oyster sauce, sprinkle with white pepper, and serve.

囍

PREP TIME: 15 MINUTES

COOK TIME: 1 HOUR 10 MINUTES

SERVES: 4

12345 SPARERIBS

1½ pounds pork spareribs, uncooked and cut into 2-inch bone-in pieces (see Cook's Note)

2 tablespoons Shaoxing Chinese cooking wine

6 tablespoons Chinkiang vinegar (or rice vinegar)

4 tablespoons light soy sauce

½ cup granulated sugar

This dish never fails to be everyone's favorite. My mom always said that the only difficult part of making these ribs is finding the balance between sweet and savory. During some kitchen experimenting one day, she discovered a nifty, easy-to-remember way to make the mix for the sauce. If you can count to five, then you can make this! Ready? Get your tablespoon out: 1 cooking wine, 2 soy sauce, 3 vinegar, 4 sugar, 5 water. Easy, right?

Mom was so excited when she cracked the code. I don't think she realized this might be the first dish where she actually measured the ingredients! How very un-Chinese of her! But finally, it was the perfect savory-sweetness every time. She's never been stingy with sharing her recipes, so she shared it with her friends and me, and now, it seems, you! I'll tell her you said thank you.

1 • Fill a large pot with water and bring it to a boil. Add the spareribs to blanch the meat and cook for about 4 minutes. Drain and discard the water. Rinse the cooked ribs and return them to the pot. Turn the heat to medium-high and add the cooking wine, vinegar, soy sauce, sugar, and ¾ cup water, stirring to dissolve the sugar. Bring it to a boil. Lower the heat to medium-low, cover, and simmer gently until the meat is tender, 45 minutes to 1 hour, turning the ribs occasionally.

2 • Remove the cover and bring the remaining liquid to a full boil. Stir until the water is mostly evaporated and only a shiny sauce is left on the ribs, about 5 minutes.

3 • Serve hot!

COOK'S NOTE: *If you don't have a cleaver to do the job, have your butcher cut the spareribs into 2-inch pieces.*

PREP TIME: 15 MINUTES

COOK TIME: 10 MINUTES

SERVES: 4

RED-STYLE WHOLE FISH
WITH TOFU

- 1 whole fish (about 2 pounds or 10 to 12 inches long), such as tilapia or cod, scaled and gutted
- 1 tablespoon light soy sauce
- 1 tablespoon Shaoxing Chinese cooking wine
- 1 teaspoon dark or mushroom soy sauce
- 1 teaspoon granulated sugar
- ½ teaspoon ground white pepper
- 1 (1-inch) knob peeled ginger (for preparing wok)
- ½ cup vegetable oil
- 4 (¼-inch) slices peeled ginger (about the diameter of a quarter)
- 2 whole scallions, cut into thirds
- 1 (12-ounce) pack soft tofu, cut into 1- or 2-inch squares
- Cooked white rice, for serving (see page 236)

"Red cooking" is the literal translation of this dish. Some versions of it can be quite red in appearance, but every Chinese family has their own way of cooking it. I attempted to make this many times over the years and never got the hang of it—I couldn't get the timing or technique exactly right so that the fish wouldn't stick to the wok. The skin would adhere to the metal, and when I flipped the fish, the skin would rip away, leaving a naked, ugly fish in my wok. The stuff of nightmares, right?

Finally, I caved and asked my mom to teach me. Can you believe that one little step I missed was the reason for all my fish failures?! All you have to do is rub some fresh ginger onto a heated wok—the fish will flip beautifully with skin intact. So, now you know. Don't forget the ginger or you'll end up with a fish that's a streaker.

1 • Make sure all the scales are removed from the fish. Slice off the fins, the back spike, and most of the tail. Rinse the inside of the fish and also rinse the blood from the inside of the head area. This will make the fish taste better and less fishy. Dry the fish thoroughly inside and out. Set aside.

2 • In a small bowl, combine 1 cup of water with the light soy sauce, cooking wine, dark or mushroom soy sauce, sugar, and white pepper. Set aside.

3 • Heat a clean wok over high heat and run a piece of ginger over the entire interior surface of the wok. This will help the wok be more nonstick. Add the oil and then SLOWLY add the whole fish. Turn the heat down to medium and cook until a light crust forms on the bottom, about 5 minutes. Resist the urge to move the fish while it cooks. Carefully spoon the hot oil over the fish if it's not submerged. Gently flip the fish and cook the other side for 5 minutes. It's best to flip the fish in the direction away from you and be very careful with the hot oil.

(RECIPE CONTINUES)

4 • Add the 4 slices of ginger and scallions and cook, stirring, to infuse the oil with the seasoning, for about 3 minutes.

5 • Add the sauce and turn up the heat to bring the liquid to a boil. Add the tofu and reduce the heat to medium-low. Cover and simmer to thicken the sauce and infuse the tofu with flavor, about 3 more minutes.

6 • Serve hot. It's even more delicious when eaten with rice.

COOK'S NOTE: *You need the fish skin for the flavor in this dish, so if you decide to use fillets instead of the whole fish, just keep the skin intact. The cook time would be 2 to 3 minutes on each side for fillets.*

PREP TIME: 15 MINUTES

COOK TIME: 20 MINUTES

SERVES: 4

CAULIFLOWER CURRY
WITH CHESTNUTS

FOR THE MARINADE:

1 tablespoon oyster sauce

½ tablespoon Shaoxing Chinese cooking wine

½ tablespoon golden curry powder, such as S&B

1 teaspoon mushroom bouillon powder

½ teaspoon kosher salt

FOR THE CURRY:

1½ tablespoons vegetable oil, divided

1 medium sweet potato, peeled and cut into ½-inch cubes

1 yellow onion, diced

1 medium head cauliflower, cut into 1-inch pieces

2 medium carrots, peeled and chopped

1 garlic clove, sliced in half

2 (¼-inch) slices peeled ginger (about the diameter of a quarter)

½ teaspoon kosher salt

3 cups hot water, divided

1 (14-ounce) can vegetable broth

The amazing thing about curry is that it acts as a wonderful base for experimentation. Throw what you want into it, like different veggies or proteins, and it'll still come out great. For example, my mom always made her chestnut curry with chicken (see page 55), but when my husband and I wanted to eat less meat, we were still able to have a satisfying meal even though we omitted the chicken. The balance of sweet and spicy with the creaminess of the curry sauce makes this a filling, "mmm"-inducing meal.

1 • **MAKE THE MARINADE:** In a small bowl, stir the oyster sauce, cooking wine, curry powder, bouillon, and salt together into a paste. Set aside.

2 • **MAKE THE CURRY:** Heat a wok over medium-high heat. Add ½ tablespoon of the oil, then add the sweet potato and cook, stirring constantly, for 2½ minutes. Remove and set aside. Add the remaining 1 tablespoon of the oil, then add the onion and cook, stirring constantly, for 3 minutes. Remove and set aside.

3 • Add the cauliflower and marinade and cook, stirring constantly, for 2 minutes. Add the carrots, garlic, ginger, and salt, and continue to stir-fry for another minute. Remove the vegetables and set aside.

(RECIPE & INGREDIENTS CONTINUE)

1 bouillon square yellow curry paste, such as S&B Golden Curry

2 teaspoons cornstarch mixed with 2 teaspoons of water

1 teaspoon granulated sugar

⅛ teaspoon ground white pepper

2 tablespoons canned whole-fat coconut milk (unsweetened)

1 (5-ounce) bag peeled roasted chestnuts

Cooked white rice, for serving (see page 236)

4 • Return the sweet potato to the wok, add 2 cups of the hot water, and allow it to simmer, covered, for 5 minutes.

5 • Remove the lid and add the cauliflower and carrots back to the wok. Stir in the vegetable broth, curry paste, cornstarch slurry, sugar, and white pepper. Allow it to simmer until all the vegetables are cooked and the gravy has formed, about 5 minutes.

6 • Stir in the onion, coconut milk, and chestnuts. If the gravy is too thick and needs more water, add the remaining hot water ¼ cup at a time. Taste-test and add more salt or curry to your preference. Once the gravy is smooth and not too thick, turn off the heat.

7 • Serve with rice!

PREP TIME: 10 MINUTES

COOK TIME: 15 MINUTES

SERVES: 4

MOM'S SPECIAL SHRIMP
WITH ASPARAGUS

18 ounces large (31/40) raw shrimp, shelled and deveined

1 tablespoon plus 1 teaspoon cornstarch, divided

1 teaspoon kosher salt, divided

12 ounces or 1 bunch of asparagus

1 cup plus 1 tablespoon vegetable oil, divided

1 tablespoon water

Asparagus wasn't a vegetable we were familiar with growing up in Hong Kong, but my mom was intrepid—after we moved to America, asparagus landed on our plates along with her signature shrimp.

With the Chinese, food is often about texture just as much as seasoning. Eating is a physical, felt experience. Like silken tofu versus firm, we like everything very *huá*, or slippery. Mom says poaching the shrimp makes them more tender and yet still able to retain a bit of crunch.

1 • Rinse the shrimp with water. Drain them and place in a medium bowl with ½ tablespoon of the cornstarch, massaging it gently into the shrimp to further clean them. Rinse the shrimp again with clean, cold water. Repeat the cleaning process with another ½ tablespoon of cornstarch and drain the water. Add ½ teaspoon of the salt and massage it into the shrimp. Then add the remaining 1 teaspoon of cornstarch and toss to coat. Set aside for 5 to 10 minutes.

2 • Rinse the asparagus and cut off and discard the tough ends. Chop the remaining stalks on the bias into 2-inch segments.

3 • In a small pot, heat 1 cup of the oil over medium-high heat for 2 to 3 minutes. Then turn off the heat and test the oil temperature with a couple of shrimp. If the oil is sizzling the shrimp vigorously, remove the shrimp and wait a minute for the oil to cool slightly. You want to poach the shrimp in hot oil but not fry them. When the oil is ready, put all the shrimp into the oil and poach until the shrimp curl and turn pink, about 2 minutes, turning the shrimp if necessary. Remove the shrimp with a strainer and transfer to a bowl.

4 • Add the remaining 1 tablespoon of the oil to a wok set over medium-high heat. Add the asparagus and cook, stirring, for 1 minute. Splash with 1 tablespoon of water and add the remaining ½ teaspoon salt and continue to stir-fry until tender, about 3 minutes. Add the shrimp and continue to cook, stirring, for about 30 seconds. Serve hot.

BABY BOK CHOY
WITH TOFU

PREP TIME: 10 MINUTES

COOK TIME: 10 MINUTES

SERVES: 4

Bok choy and tofu is a classic Chinese dish and a restaurant staple. Think of it kind of like a side salad, as we pair it with our main courses so often. My mother often serves it simply because it's easy to make. She likes to prepare it "clean," as she says, with just salt and oil, but I prefer to have a bit more flavor. It's quick to make if you're hungry and you need some healthy food fast. I actually get upset if I don't have bok choy and tofu ready to go in my refrigerator! Plus, it's refreshing to serve cold the next day. (Though I personally don't do that—the Chinese do not believe in eating meals cold, so I always reheat it. You can't do that with leftover arugula!)

½ cup sliced dried wood ear mushrooms (optional)

1 tablespoon vegetable oil

8 heads baby bok choy, rinsed and chopped into 1½-inch pieces

1 tablespoon oyster sauce

½ teaspoon kosher salt

12 ounces silken firm tofu, cut into 1-inch cubes

½ cup chicken broth

2 teaspoons cornstarch mixed with 2 teaspoons water

1 • In a medium bowl, soak the mushrooms (if using) in water until they are rehydrated. If you don't like the flavor, you can skip this ingredient.

2 • In a deep frying pan or wok over medium-high heat, heat the vegetable oil. Add the bok choy and cook, stirring constantly, until it is bright green and slightly softened, about 3 minutes. Add the oyster sauce and salt and mix well. Add the tofu, chicken broth, and mushrooms (if using) and bring to a gentle boil. Stir in the cornstarch slurry to create a little gravy, then immediately turn off the heat.

3 • Serve as a side or main dish.

COOK'S NOTE: *One of the things my mother always says is to make sure your vegetables are pretty much cooked before adding the salt, because the salt extracts the water from the vegetables and changes the texture—and sometimes it can make the vegetables tougher. So, you cook the vegetables until they're just about to the tenderness that you want, and then you add the salt.*

DIM SUM GAI-LAN

PREP TIME: 5 MINUTES

COOK TIME: 5 MINUTES

SERVES: 2 TO 4 AS A SIDE DISH

1 bunch gai-lan (or Chinese broccoli)

2 teaspoons vegetable oil

2 teaspoons kosher salt

2 tablespoons oyster sauce

Gai-lan is always on the menu whenever we go out to dim sum with my mom in Hong Kong. I love seeing the waiters roll the food carts over to our table and explain their wares. We pick what we want, then the waiters plunk down the piping-hot dishes on the lazy Susan in the middle of the table. The gai-lan, or Chinese broccoli in oyster sauce, is a perfect accompaniment to the dumplings and other dishes.

I love that most everyone has tried dim sum, or at least knows what it is. A restaurant during dim sum time is always fun and loud—almost like going to a sporting event, with everyone at your table competing (good-naturedly) for food. And if you're a party of one or two, often Chinese restaurants will seat you with total strangers at big tables of eight. Don't worry—nobody minds, and your server will know to give your party its own bill. That said, going with a large group is always better because then you get to try more dishes. So, consider bringing family and friends to dim sum rather than a date—unless they can eat a *lot*!

1 • Rinse the gai-lan and peel off the tough parts of the stalks. Cut about ½ inch off the ends.

2 • Fill a large pot with water and bring to boil. Add the oil and salt to the water. Add the gai-lan and boil until they are bright, dark green, and tender, 4 to 5 minutes. Remove and drip-drain the broccoli, then pile it neatly on a plate.

3 • Drizzle the oyster sauce over the gai-lan and serve hot.

SILKY STEAMED EGGS

PREP TIME: 5 MINUTES

COOK TIME: 10 MINUTES

SERVES: 4

Boy, I remember making this so many nights when I was shooting in Vancouver. I was on a series called *Stargate Universe*, living alone, separated from my family. This became my go-to meal when I just wanted something warm, comforting, and quick.

Mom says these eggs should be "slippery," which makes sense, as that is the literal translation from Chinese for this dish. If your steamed eggs are very stiff or curdled, then you've overcooked them. My mom's trick to ensure that the eggs don't overcook is to put a plate over the bowl as they steam. A generational favorite!

4 to 5 large eggs

Warm water (or chicken broth for more flavor)

½ teaspoon light soy sauce

½ teaspoon kosher salt

1 teaspoon minced chives (optional)

2 drops sesame oil (optional)

Cooked white rice, for serving (optional, see page 236)

1 • Set up a large steamer using a heatproof rack, trivet, or steamer insert in a large pot with a tight-fitting lid. Add water to the pot until it reaches just below the rack's surface, usually 1 to 2 inches deep.

2 • In a liquid measuring cup, whisk the eggs. To a heatproof bowl that can fit in the steamer, add 1½ times the volume of the eggs of warm water or warm chicken broth. (For example: If the eggs equal 1 cup, add 1½ cups warm water.) Add the light soy sauce and salt and mix well but gently to avoid air bubbles.

3 • Cover the bowl with a plate or plastic wrap to prevent too much of the hot steam from making contact with the eggs directly, as it will cause a skin to form. If you're using plastic wrap, pierce it with a knife in several places to allow the moisture from the eggs to escape as they cook.

4 • Over medium-high heat, bring the water in the pot to a boil. Put the bowl on top of the rack. Cover the pot and steam the egg mixture over medium heat, maintaining a simmer, until a custard texture is achieved, 12 to 15 minutes, adding more water if needed. Lift the cover and test the eggs by cutting into them with a knife; if they "bleed" runny or watery, then steam for another 5 minutes. You can also add chives on top at this point, if desired.

5 • Carefully remove the hot bowl. Serve the eggs immediately, drizzled with sesame oil, if using. They're great over rice, if desired.

GARLICKY SPINACH

PREP TIME: 5 MINUTES

COOK TIME: 5 MINUTES

SERVES: 2 TO 4

1 tablespoon vegetable oil

1 (10-ounce) pack baby spinach or 2 bunches of spinach, chopped

6 garlic cloves, chopped or sliced

1 teaspoon Shaoxing Chinese cooking wine

¼ teaspoon kosher salt

⅛ teaspoon ground white pepper

½ teaspoon black bean and garlic sauce (optional)

I absolutely can't live without my spinach. Okay, maybe that's a slight exaggeration, but I do love cooking it because I'm always a bit anemic, and spinach is a great source of iron. Unlike many Americans whose veggies consist of salads, we love to cook ours. My mother has never understood why Americans eat so much salad. She'd say, "Why is everyone eating what cows eat?!" For the Chinese, eating raw vegetables can be considered unhealthy because they can cause bloating and other gastric issues. And with increasingly common reports of *E. coli* outbreaks from raw vegetables, I'd say my mom was right. Eat your (cooked!) vegetables, kids.

Heat the vegetable oil in a large skillet or wok over medium heat. Add the spinach and garlic and cook, stirring constantly, for 3 minutes. Splash with the cooking wine and stir in the salt and white pepper. For a more robust flavor, toss the spinach with the black bean and garlic sauce, if desired.

PREP TIME: 5 MINUTES

COOK TIME: 5 MINUTES

SERVES: 4

CHINESE CHIVES WITH EGGS

6 large eggs

4 tablespoons vegetable oil, divided

1 teaspoon kosher salt, divided

1 bunch Chinese chives, sliced into 1½-inch pieces

1 teaspoon Shaoxing Chinese cooking wine

A lot of people are surprised when I tell them that my kids loved to devour this dish, even when they were little. Well, they're not so little anymore! Michaela is living and working in New York City, and Cooper's in college in San Francisco. I enjoy being an empty nester with my husband now, but at the same time, I miss my kids so much. Whenever they come home for a visit, I know they'll request this dish. I buy the Chinese chives ahead of their arrival and am always happy to prepare it for them. Moms know best!

In fact, my daughter was upset when she didn't see this dish on the list to be photographed for the book. She insisted that this recipe should be accompanied by a photo. Of course I couldn't say no, so you have Michaela to thank for the beautiful photo.

1 • In a medium bowl, whisk the eggs, then set aside.

2 • Heat 2 tablespoons of the vegetable oil in a wok over high heat, then turn it down to medium-high heat. Stir ½ teaspoon of the salt into the oil. Add the chives and cook, stirring constantly, until the chives begin to become tender, taking care not to overcook, as they can become tough, 1 to 2 minutes. Remove the wok from the heat and set aside.

3 • Carefully scrape or wipe the wok clean. Add the remaining 2 tablespoons of the oil to the wok over high heat, then turn it down to medium-high heat, swirling it to coat the bottom. Add the eggs and cook, stirring constantly and chopping into bite-size pieces as you stir, until they are almost finished cooking, about 2 minutes. Pour the cooking wine into the wok using a swirling motion around the side edge of the pan so that it seeps evenly into the eggs. Add the remaining ½ teaspoon of the salt and stir to incorporate the seasonings. Add the chives and cook, stirring, to warm through, about 1 minute. Serve hot.

COOK'S NOTE: *Never let chives sit in the fridge to the point of rotting—you will think that something died in the refrigerator, and it will stink up your house every time you open the refrigerator door. Use them within a day or two of purchase.*

SHAVED ICE
WITH SWEET RED BEANS

PREP TIME: 10 MINUTES
PLUS 5 HOURS SOAKING TIME

COOK TIME: 5½ HOURS

SERVES: 8

SWEET RED BEANS:

2 cups dried Chinese red beans (hong dou in Chinese, azuki in Japanese)

1 cup granulated sugar

SHAVED ICE DESSERT:

2 cups shaved ice per serving

2 tablespoons condensed milk per serving

CRUSHED ICE DRINK:

2 cups crushed ice per serving

2 tablespoons condensed milk per serving

1 cup evaporated milk or soy milk per serving

Chinese cuisine is not usually known for its desserts. Dessert often consists of fruit or warm tapioca in a slightly sweet broth or perhaps some kind of bun stuffed with a semisweet filling. When I lived in Hong Kong as a kid, my favorite dessert was shaved ice with sweet red beans. Super refreshing, it was sort of like our version of ice cream. Five decades later, it's still one of my favorites.

A few years back, I surprised my mom by making this from scratch (it's not hard but it does take time). Now, whenever she visits, she asks me for red bean ice like a little kid. Talk about role reversal! I absolutely love making it for her, though. I think it takes her back to her own childhood, too. Every time I make it for her, it feels like a special trip to Chinatown with Mom.

1 • **MAKE THE SWEET RED BEANS:** Rinse the dried red beans and soak them, submerged in a bowl of water, for 5 hours or overnight.

2 • Drain the beans and place them in a pot with 4 cups of water. Bring the beans to a boil over high heat and continue to boil, with the pot partially covered, for 10 minutes.

3 • If more than half of the water has evaporated, add 2 cups of hot water. Lower the heat to medium-low and simmer the beans, completely covered, until they are softened, 1 to 1½ hours. Make sure the water always covers the beans, adding more hot water ½ cup at a time to ensure the beans do not burn. Once the beans are softened, add the sugar and mix well. If you'd like to boil off some of the extra water, continue to cook, stirring constantly, until you have a thicker consistency, almost like a sweet, thick chili. Alternatively, if you prefer your beans to be less thick in consistency, you can use a slotted spoon to remove the beans before the final boil. Remove the beans from the heat.

(RECIPE CONTINUES)

4 • Once the beans are cooled, refrigerate them in a sealed container. The red beans can also be frozen and used as needed. Use an ice cube tray to freeze small portion sizes of the red beans or use a larger tray for ⅓-cup or ½-cup portions.

5 • **FOR THE SHAVED ICE DESSERT:** It's easy to find inexpensive ice shavers to make shaved ice desserts. Freeze the round tubs of water that fit into the plastic ice shavers or use a blender that can make shaved ice. Put about 2 cups of shaved ice in a bowl, then add the cold red beans and top with the condensed milk. Fresh or canned fruits of choice can also be added.

6 • **FOR THE CRUSHED ICE DRINK:** In a tall glass, add the cold red beans, crushed ice, condensed milk (to taste), then enough evaporated milk or milk of choice. Stir and drink with a spoon and a straw.

RESTAURANT CLASSICS

Welcome to the Chinatown Inn—our family's restaurant in Pittsburgh, and the place that shaped so much of my youth (and, honestly, my palate). It was founded in 1943, established by Tong Yee, Baba's father, and is the only remaining business of what was once a bustling Chinatown in downtown Pittsburgh.

In 2022, a historical marker was installed in front, an honor bestowed by the Pennsylvania Historical and Museum Commission. Today, my brother Jonathan and his wife, Wei, still run the restaurant, keeping the woks hot and the regulars happy with beef and broccoli, shrimp fried rice, wonton soup—those comforting, reliable dishes that generations of customers have loved and ordered again and again. Of course, growing up, as I mentioned before, we'd often eat dishes that were not found on the menu, what we might call more authentic Chinese dishes. I always enjoyed the ritual of family and staff gathering together after the lunch rush and digging into food that either my father or one of the chefs had whipped up just for us. We might have, for example, tomatoes and beef, fried rice with Chinese sausage, silken steamed eggs, or winter melon soup.

When I sat down to write this book, I felt a little hesitant to include some of our well-guarded secret restaurant recipes, but I decided it was the only way to truly represent and share that part of my childhood with you. Of course, many of the restaurant's recipes were not written down (classic Chinese family move when it comes to cooking—we go by instinct, not measuring cups), so I had to re-create some of them from memory. There was a lot of trial and error and lots of taste testing. (Confession: I definitely gained weight working on this cookbook, but it

1. (previous page) Here I am with my brother, hanging out at the restaurant in front of Christmas cards taped onto the wall. (I probably did that decorating!) There's a stack of restaurant menus in front of us.
2. A birthday celebration at the restaurant—this time it was my turn, at about fifteen. (The guy in the back is a customer!)
3. Another birthday party at the Chinatown Inn, with the customers! (You get the picture; we were ALWAYS there.) I was in high school here, and I wonder what was in that box . . .
4. Here we all are at our wedding reception at the restauraunt in Pittsburgh, after our traditional Chinese ceremony in 1995.
5. I hung out at the bar in the restaurant a lot as a teenager because that was where the TV was. I also learned how to make drinks for customers. All hands on deck!

was worth every extra inch on my waistline because the dishes turned out great.) It's as if the recipes were magically embedded in me on a cellular level. This endeavor has turned out to be a poignant walk down memory lane through my taste buds.

I feel a greater sense of pride now for being a restaurant daughter and have a renewed love and appreciation for the Chinatown Inn. This takeaway (haha, get the pun?) certainly is very different from what I felt as a kid working there. I couldn't wait to get away from the restaurant. Sometimes I thought of it as another child that my parents paid more attention to than my brothers and me. Running a restaurant is no joke. My parents worked seven days a week, barely taking a breath for holidays—maybe two or three days off a year, *max*. It was exhausting, intense, and full of love and energy. The restaurant wasn't just our livelihood, it was our life. Writing this cookbook has made me realize how much the Inn gave to my family and the community.

Hey, if you visit Pittsburgh, stop by in person! Treat yourself to our delicious shrimp egg rolls. And don't forget to glance at the wall next to the register—my brother has a mini shrine of photos from my acting career proudly displayed there. It's very sweet (and slightly embarrassing). Love you, big brother.

1. Eric and me visiting the restaurant in the early 1990s.
2. The most recent Chinatown Inn takeout menu.
3. The historical facade of the Chinatown Inn, today.
4. Lots of delicious dishes behind this menu cover.

PREP TIME: 10 MINUTES

COOK TIME: 5 MINUTES

SERVES: 6

EGG DROP SOUP

2 large eggs plus 2 egg whites, divided

2 tablespoons cornstarch

4 cups homemade chicken stock

1 whole scallion, chopped, divided

1 teaspoon kosher salt

½ teaspoon ground white pepper

½ teaspoon mushroom bouillon powder (optional)

¼ teaspoon turmeric powder (optional)

Pinch granulated sugar

½ teaspoon sesame oil

Egg drop soup is one of the restaurant's most common lunch orders, right alongside wonton soup. A lot of people have a hard time making it—they can't seem to get the egg ribbons or the consistency right. It's something that seems like it would be simple to make, but there's an art form to it. You want it to be viscous, but you don't want it to be too thick, as I've found a lot of restaurants make the mistake of doing. Another factor in making egg drop soup a success is the quality of your broth. Our restaurant makes its stock from scratch every day, and the incredible flavor it adds to the soup is revelatory. So, I hope this recipe helps you to master the art of egg drop. Use your favorite stock, and remember—you have to break a few eggs to make an ~~omelet~~ egg drop soup!

1 • In measuring cups, lightly beat the 2 whole eggs and, separately, the egg whites. Set aside.

2 • In a small bowl, mix the cornstarch with ¼ cup water until completely blended. Set aside.

3 • In a medium pot over medium heat, bring the stock to a simmer. Add half of the scallions, the salt, white pepper, mushroom bouillon powder (if desired), turmeric powder (if desired), and sugar. Whisk in the cornstarch mixture, making sure no lumps are formed. Raise the heat to high and bring the stock to a boil, then turn off the heat.

4 • Stir the broth with one hand and, with the other hand, slowly drizzle the beaten whole eggs into the broth, then drizzle in the egg whites to create strands or "flowers" of egg. Add the sesame oil.

5 • Ladle the soup into small bowls and garnish with the remaining scallions. Serve hot.

PREP TIME: 20 MINUTES PLUS 15 MINUTES MARINATING TIME

COOK TIME: 10 MINUTES

MAKES 30 TO 40 WONTONS

SIMPLE WONTON SOUP

2 tablespoons light soy sauce (plus more for serving, optional)

1 teaspoon kosher salt

1 teaspoon ground white pepper

1 pound ground meat (pork, chicken, or turkey)

1 (12-ounce) package thick, square wonton wrappers

1 large egg, beaten

Chili sauce (optional)

1 (14.5-ounce) can chicken broth, or about 2 cups homemade stock

1 whole scallion, chopped

If the thought of making traditional wontons like Popo's Wontons (page 34) overwhelms you, don't panic—I've got you covered. This recipe for wontons cuts some corners without losing any flavor. At the restaurant, we make wontons using this method because it's so much faster—Americans love their wontons, so we need to have a *lot* on hand. Plus, these wontons don't include shrimp, so those with allergies or an aversion to shellfish can eat them. FYI, these are also great as party apps. Because they use thicker wonton wrappers, you can deep-fry them and they'll hold their shape beautifully.

1 • In a medium nonreactive bowl, combine the soy sauce, salt, and white pepper. Add the meat and mix well with the seasoning. Set aside to marinate for 15 minutes in the refrigerator.

2 • Place a ½-tablespoon dollop of marinated meat above the bottom corner of a wonton skin, leaving about ¼ inch of space to the edge of the wrapper. Using a butter knife, fold the corner up and over the knife and meat. Roll the wonton skin once with the knife, then slip the knife out. The wonton should be a triangle with meat inside.

3 • Dip the knife into the beaten egg and dab the egg on the right point of the triangle. Fold over to the opposite point of the triangle and squeeze to seal it with the egg. Repeat with the remaining wontons. (See Cook's Note if you are freezing the wontons.)

4 • When ready to eat, bring a large pot of water to a boil, leaving enough room in the pot for 1 to 2 cups of additional water. Add the wontons. When the water boils again, add ½ cup of cold water. When the water boils a third time, add another ½ cup of cold water. When the wontons float to the top, they are done. Adding cold water in steps like this keeps the skin of the wontons from overcooking and becoming too soft.

(RECIPE CONTINUES)

5 • You can eat these alone with some soy sauce or chili sauce, if desired.

6 • To make a simple wonton soup, boil 2 cups of chicken broth. Serve the broth in small bowls, add the cooked wontons, and garnish with the scallion.

COOK'S NOTE: *To freeze the wontons: On a tray or plate lined with parchment paper, place the wontons in rows, with a bit of separation between them so that they do not stick together. Make sure the tray or plate will fit in your freezer. Once the tray is full, freeze the wontons until the skin feels solid and frozen, about 1 hour. You can then place the wontons in plastic freezer bags without worrying about them sticking together. Immediately place the bags back in the freezer to further freeze the wontons. Remember to write a date on the bags. They will keep for 3 to 4 months.*

To cook frozen wontons, repeat the above, but add ½ cup cold water one more time because the frozen meat needs a bit longer to cook through.

PREP TIME: 45 MINUTES

COOK TIME: 30 MINUTES

MAKES 18 TO 20 EGG ROLLS

THE BEST EGG ROLLS

FOR THE FILLING:

3 teaspoons light soy sauce, divided

5 tablespoons vegetable oil, divided

1 tablespoon cornstarch, divided

¼ teaspoon dark mushroom soy sauce

1 pound ground meat (pork, chicken, or turkey)

12 ounces large (31/40) raw shrimp, shelled and deveined

2½ teaspoons kosher salt, divided

1 cup finely chopped yellow onion

2 cups finely chopped cabbage

3 cups finely chopped celery

¼ teaspoon ground white pepper

½ teaspoon mushroom or vegetable bouillon powder

3 tablespoons creamy natural peanut butter (if allergic, swap for another seed or nut butter)

Our egg rolls, stuffed with meat and vegetables, are one of the restaurant's specialties. It's definitely a main attraction for all our repeat customers. Forget those wimpy, thin egg rolls the size of spring rolls—never at the Chinatown Inn, nor in my house! I always have some in my freezer, and I've made them with both ground turkey and pork, so use whichever protein you like best. And no, peanut butter did not accidentally make its way into the recipe's ingredient list—it's the secret weapon to achieving the creaminess in the filling, and it gives the egg rolls a nice, subtly nutty flavor. If you're allergic to peanuts, swap out for any other nut butter.

SIDE NOTE: "Duck sauce" is a term that stuck long after Chinese American restaurants originally started serving this sweet plum- or apricot-flavored sauce alongside their duck dishes. It's now a standard condiment used across the United States and is especially nice with egg rolls.

1 • MAKE THE FILLING: In a medium nonreactive bowl, combine 2 teaspoons of the light soy sauce, 1 teaspoon of the vegetable oil, ½ tablespoon of the cornstarch, and the dark mushroom soy sauce. Add the ground meat, mix well, and set aside in the refrigerator.

2 • Massage the shrimp with the remaining ½ tablespoon of cornstarch, then rinse well with cold water. Transfer to a bowl, add ½ teaspoon of the salt, and marinate the shrimp in the refrigerator for 15 minutes. Then chop the raw shrimp into small pieces.

3 • Heat a large wok over high heat and add 2 tablespoons of the oil. Add the seasoned ground meat and cook, stirring frequently, until the meat is browned, about 5 minutes. Remove the meat from the wok and set aside.

(RECIPE & INGREDIENTS CONTINUE)

TSINGTAO

FOR THE DUCK SAUCE:

1 cup applesauce

⅓ cup apricot jam

2½ tablespoons white vinegar

3 teaspoons rice vinegar

1 teaspoon light soy sauce

⅛ teaspoon dark mushroom soy sauce (for color)

FOR THE CHINESE MUSTARD:

2 tablespoons Chinese mustard powder

FOR THE EGG ROLLS:

1 (16-ounce) package egg roll wraps

1 large egg, beaten with 1 tablespoon water

2 to 3 cups vegetable, corn, or peanut oil for frying

4 • Lower the temperature to medium-high and add 2 more tablespoons of the oil. Add the onion and cook, stirring constantly, until tender, 3 to 5 minutes. Add the cabbage and celery, the remaining 2 teaspoons salt, the white pepper, and the mushroom bouillon powder. To keep the vegetables on the drier side, spread them out in the wok to help the water evaporate. Cook until the vegetables begin to soften but are still crunchy, not wilted, about 5 minutes.

5 • Turn off the heat. Spread the vegetables around the side of the wok, leaving the center open. Drizzle in the peanut butter, spreading as evenly as possible over the vegetables.

6 • Return the heat to medium-high and add the remaining 2 teaspoons of oil and the shrimp to the center of the wok. Cook the shrimp, stirring constantly, until pink, 2 to 3 minutes, then mix well with the vegetables. Add the cooked ground meat and mix well. Add more salt and pepper to taste.

7 • Spread the mixture on a baking tray or large platter to cool. Once cool enough, cover the filling with plastic wrap or foil, then put it into the refrigerator until ready to wrap.

8 • MAKE THE DUCK SAUCE: In a medium bowl, mix together the applesauce, apricot jam, white vinegar, rice vinegar, light soy sauce, and mushroom soy sauce. Refrigerate the duck sauce until you're ready to serve the egg rolls.

9 • MAKE THE MUSTARD SAUCE: In a small bowl, add 2 tablespoons water to the mustard powder and mix well. The mustard does not need to be refrigerated. Set aside.

(RECIPE CONTINUES)

10 • TO ASSEMBLE THE EGG ROLLS: Place one egg roll wrapper with a corner pointing toward you. Add about 3 tablespoons of filling to the center of the wrapper, about 2 inches above the corner. Roll the corner over the filling and gently tuck it under the filling, keeping slight pressure so that the wrap will be tight. Brush the egg wash to the right and left edges and over the remaining unrolled parts of the wrapper. Fold right and left corners over the top of the egg roll stuffing, then continue rolling the wrapper toward the opposite corner. Make sure not to tear the wrapper. If it does tear, you can use the egg wash to close it or you can add a small piece of another egg roll wrapper and use the egg wash to cover and seal the tear. Place the roll on a sheet pan lined with parchment paper. Repeat.

11 • Heat 2 to 3 cups of oil in a wok over medium-high heat until the temperature reaches 300° to 350°F. If you do not have a thermometer, then watch the oil heat until it slightly bubbles on the side of the wok or some steam is seen.

12 • Gently place 3 to 4 egg rolls one at a time in the hot oil to deep fry. Turn them once one side browns. Adjust the heat to maintain the frying oil temperature. Remove the egg rolls to a rack set over a sheet pan to drain the oil.

13 • Serve the egg rolls with duck sauce and mustard sauce.

14 • The duck sauce and Chinese mustard will keep for a week or longer.

COOK'S NOTE: *Egg rolls will keep for about 5 days in the refrigerator. They also freeze well; just wrap each egg roll in foil before freezing. Reheat the egg rolls on a rack in an air fryer at 400°F for 3 to 4 minutes if they've been refrigerated, and for 8 minutes if they were frozen. The air-frying will cause the excess oil in the egg rolls to drip, which will make them less greasy, lighter, and crispier. Air-frying egg rolls after deep-frying works great if you're not serving them immediately after deep-frying.*

PREP TIME: 15 MINUTES

COOK TIME: 15 MINUTES

SERVES: 4

BEEF AND BROCCOLI

2 tablespoons plus 2 teaspoons vegetable oil, divided

2 teaspoons cornstarch

1 teaspoon light soy sauce

½ teaspoon dark mushroom soy sauce

8 ounces flank steak, thinly sliced

2 (¼-inch) slices peeled ginger (about the diameter of a quarter)

1 scallion, white and green parts, chopped

1 (16-ounce) broccoli crown, separated into bite-size florets

½ cup plus 2 tablespoons water or chicken broth, divided

1 tablespoon black bean and garlic sauce

½ tablespoon oyster sauce

½ teaspoon kosher salt

½ tablespoon cornstarch mixed with 1 tablespoon water

Such a classic restaurant recipe, beef and broccoli is a dish that you must add to your repertoire—it's simple, easy, and quick. Think of it as a more Americanized version of our beef and bok choy. Broccoli became an easy-access staple for Chinese restaurants to source, which is why it became so ubiquitous across the country. It played an important role in American food culture because it introduced vegetables as a significant part of the main entree, rather than just as side dishes. This is so much better than the sad, soft steamed broccoli of the past, don't you think?

I think this dish represents the whole journey of this cookbook rather well. Beef and broccoli is truly Chinese American, blending the two cultures into a delicious and popular dish. Now, I'm not calling myself a delicious dish, but I think that's why we chose it for the cover.

1 • In a medium nonreactive bowl, combine 2 teaspoons of the vegetable oil, the cornstarch, light soy sauce, and mushroom soy sauce. Add the steak and coat well with the seasoning.

2 • Add 1 tablespoon of the oil to a wok over high heat. Add the steak, ginger, and scallion. Leave the steak slices on one side to sear for about 30 seconds, then flip them and sear the other sides. Cook, stirring constantly, for 1 minute, then remove the steak from the heat and set aside.

3 • Add the remaining 1 tablespoon of oil to the wok and add the broccoli. Add 2 tablespoons of the water and cook, stirring constantly, until the broccoli turns bright green, 2 to 3 minutes. Add the black bean and garlic sauce, oyster sauce, and salt and cook, stirring, for 2 minutes.

(RECIPE CONTINUES)

4 • Add the steak back in and stir to combine. Add the remaining water while pushing the veggies and meat to the sides of the wok. When the liquid comes to a boil, add the cornstarch slurry, stirring to create a gravy, then turn off the heat. Mix the gravy together with the meat and broccoli and transfer to a plate.

COOK'S NOTES: *Feel free to add more water or broth if, like my kids, you prefer more gravy. And if you prefer more meat, ensure that it will sear properly by cooking it in two batches, wiping the wok clean in between and adding more oil.*

Ginger shouldn't be refrigerated. A lot of people make that mistake. The moisture gets into the root and causes mold. Weird that you can find it in the refrigerated section of supermarkets. Even if you see the mold on the outside and cut it off, it might not be fine; it may have already traveled through the ginger and you just don't see it. You can grow your own, too—it's kinda fun. Just buy it from the supermarket, stick it in some dirt with a bit of sand on top, and watch it root and grow!

PREP TIME: 20 MINUTES

COOK TIME: 15 HOURS

SERVES: 4

CRISPY CHOW MEIN
WITH PORK

- 4 tablespoons plus 2 teaspoons vegetable oil, divided
- 1 (15-ounce) package fresh, thin Chinese chow mein egg noodles (see Cook's Notes)
- 2 teaspoons light soy sauce, divided
- ½ teaspoon dark mushroom soy sauce
- 1 teaspoon cornstarch
- 8 ounces pork loin, sliced into thin strips (see Cook's Notes)
- 1 (¼-inch) slice peeled ginger (about the diameter of a quarter)
- 1 whole scallion, cut into thirds
- ½ yellow onion, thinly sliced
- ½ head cabbage, shredded
- 1 carrot, thinly sliced or peeled into strips
- ½ cup chicken broth
- 2 garlic cloves, minced
- 1 teaspoon kosher salt
- ⅛ teaspoon ground white pepper
- Chili sauce, for serving (optional)

Ready for a history lesson? Hong Kong's cuisine is based mainly on the Cantonese cooking style. In the 1800s, Canton—now known as Guangzhou—became famed for its sophisticated cooking, and many Hong Kong chefs trained at Cantonese restaurants. Eventually, Cantonese cooking, which is known for its delicate, balanced flavors (rather than, say, the boldness of Sichuan cuisine) became the standard in Hong Kong.

My dad was a Hong Kong–style cook, which meant that his chow mein was a little different from the standardized chow mein. He would pan-fry his noodles, adding more texture and toasty flavor to the dish. I've always loved that extra bit of crunch that pan-frying gives the noodles.

1 • In a large sauté pan or wok over medium-high heat, heat 1 tablespoon of the oil, then add the noodles in a layer and cook until browned on the bottom, 4 or 5 minutes. Flip the noodles, add another tablespoon of the oil, and cook until golden, an additional 2 minutes. Set the noodles aside on a large serving plate—by pan frying them, you get a very crispy exterior but the center will remain soft.

2 • In a medium bowl, combine 2 teaspoons of the oil, 1 teaspoon of the light soy sauce, the mushroom soy sauce, and cornstarch. Add the pork strips, coat well with the seasoning, and set aside.

3 • Heat a large wok over medium-high heat and add 1 tablespoon of the oil. Add the ginger and scallion to flavor the oil, then add the pork strips. Let them sit for 1 minute to sear before turning them over and searing again for 1 more minute. Then cook, stirring constantly, until all sides of the pork are browned, about 1 minute. Remove the pork from the wok and set aside.

(RECIPE CONTINUES)

4 • Add the remaining tablespoon of the oil to wok, then add the onion and cook, stirring, until softened, about 2 minutes. Add the cabbage and carrot and cook, stirring constantly, for 5 minutes. Add the chicken broth, garlic, remaining teaspoon of light soy sauce, salt, and white pepper and cook, stirring constantly, until the cabbage and carrots are softened, 2 or 3 more minutes.

5 • Add the cooked pork back to the wok and cook, stirring constantly, for 2 minutes. Add additional salt and pepper to taste.

6 • Scoop the mixture on top of the crispy noodles and serve hot, immediately. It's delicious served with some Chinese chili sauce, if desired.

COOK'S NOTES: *It's easier to cut the pork into strips if it's lightly frozen. Slice the pork loin into ¼-inch slices, then lay the pieces flat and slice into ¼-inch strips.*

If you can't find fresh, thin chow mein noodles, you can purchase 6 ounces of dry, uncooked chow mein noodles. Cook them per the package directions, then rinse with cold water, drain well, and towel dry before following the directions above.

SHRIMP FRIED RICE

PREP TIME: 10 MINUTES

COOK TIME: 10 MINUTES

SERVES: 4

Of all the fried rice options at the restaurant, it's shrimp that gets ordered the most. It's the costliest protein to add, but it's also the easiest because it takes the least amount of time to cook. Over the years, I've tinkered with the restaurant's recipe to get it just to my liking. For example, my family adds more mushroom soy sauce to darken and intensify the flavor, but I use less because I like it lighter. I also add more egg and kick it up a notch by using garlic powder and white pepper. Of course, you can also adapt this as a vegetarian dish, or, if you're shellfish intolerant, use chicken or beef instead. Don't be afraid to play around—fried rice is very forgiving.

10 large (31/40) raw shrimp, shelled, deveined, and cut into thirds

½ tablespoon cornstarch mixed with 1 tablespoon water, divided

1 teaspoon kosher salt, divided

3 tablespoons vegetable oil, divided

4 large eggs, lightly beaten

1 teaspoon Shaoxing Chinese cooking wine

¼ teaspoon ground white pepper

3 cups cooked white rice, day-old or overnight (see page 236)

3 scallions, white and green parts, chopped

1 cup bean sprouts (optional)

1 tablespoon light soy sauce

1 teaspoon dark mushroom soy sauce

½ tablespoon garlic powder

Hot sauce, for serving (optional)

1 • Rinse the shrimp and drain the water. In a bowl, rub ½ tablespoon of the cornstarch slurry onto the shrimp and massage the shrimp to clean. Rinse again. Add ¼ teaspoon of the salt and ¼ teaspoon of the cornstarch slurry and rub onto the shrimp. Set aside.

2 • Heat a large wok over medium-high heat with 1 teaspoon of the vegetable oil and add the beaten eggs. Cook the eggs, stirring frequently, until they are half done, about 2 minutes, then splash with the cooking wine. Add a couple of pinches of the salt and white pepper and stir to combine. Remove the eggs from the pan and set aside. Scrape off the stuck-on egg and wipe the wok clean with paper towels, or rinse quickly and dry the wok on the stovetop.

3 • Return the wok to medium-high heat. Add 1 teaspoon of the oil and cook the shrimp, stirring constantly, until pink, 2 to 3 minutes. Remove the shrimp and set aside with the cooked eggs.

4 • Add 2 tablespoons of the oil to the wok over high heat. Toss in the overnight rice and stir and flatten it to break up any large clumps. Stir in the chopped scallions and bean sprouts, if desired. Add the light soy sauce, dark mushroom soy sauce, garlic powder, and the remaining ½ teaspoon of salt. Continue to toss the rice with the spatula to make it fluffy. Stir in the remaining teaspoon of oil and toss in the cooked shrimp and eggs. Season with salt and white pepper to taste.

5 • Serve hot. It's also stellar with some hot sauce, if desired.

SHRIMP
WITH LOBSTER SAUCE

PREP TIME: 15 MINUTES

COOK TIME: 15 HOURS

SERVES: 4

The name of this dish is a little misleading. There's not actually any lobster in this recipe—this just happens to use the same sauce as that of a popular Chinese lobster dish. Confusing, I know. I've never been able to find shrimp with lobster sauce executed well at other restaurants, so I never order it unless I'm at ours. This was one of the dishes that didn't have a written recipe, so I've re-created it from memory. Don't skimp on the shrimp—you want meaty guys, not little dinky ones. And definitely have it with rice!

FOR THE SHRIMP AND MEAT MARINADE:

15 ounces large (31/40) raw shrimp, shelled and deveined

1 tablespoon plus 1½ teaspoons cornstarch, divided

1 teaspoon kosher salt, divided

¼ teaspoon ground white pepper

¼ pound ground meat (pork or turkey)

½ teaspoon vegetable oil

FOR THE WOK:

2 tablespoons vegetable oil, divided

1 (1-inch) knob ginger, peeled and thinly sliced

3 garlic cloves, minced

1 teaspoon kosher salt

1 cup chicken broth

2 tablespoons light soy sauce

1 tablespoon Shaoxing Chinese cooking wine

½ cup frozen peas

½ teaspoon ground white pepper

½ teaspoon granulated sugar

2 tablespoons cornstarch mixed with 2 tablespoons water

1 large egg, lightly beaten

Cooked white rice, for serving (see page 236)

1 • **MAKE THE SHRIMP AND MEAT MARINADE:** Rinse the shrimp in cold water. Add 1 tablespoon of the cornstarch and massage the shrimp gently to clean. Rinse off the cornstarch. Add ½ teaspoon of the salt and 1 teaspoon of the cornstarch and mix well. Set aside.

2 • In a medium bowl, combine the remaining ½ teaspoon of the salt and the white pepper to the ground meat and mix well. Then add the vegetable oil and the remaining ½ teaspoon of the cornstarch and mix well. Set aside.

3 • **FOR THE WOK:** Heat a large wok over medium-high heat, then add 1 tablespoon of the oil. Add the ginger and then the shrimp and cook, stirring, until the shrimp is pink and almost cooked through, about 3 minutes. Remove the shrimp from the wok and set aside.

4 • With the wok still hot, add the remaining 1 tablespoon of oil. Add the ground meat, garlic, and the salt. Cook, stirring constantly, until the meat is cooked through, about 3 minutes.

5 • Add the chicken broth, soy sauce, cooking wine, peas, white pepper, and sugar. Bring the liquid to a boil, then cover the wok, reduce the heat to medium, and simmer for 3 minutes. Remove the cover and bring the sauce to a boil. Stir in the cornstarch slurry to thicken.

6 • Toss in the shrimp. Drizzle in the beaten egg while stirring everything quickly, then turn off the heat. Serve over hot rice.

VLT
Calories

PREP TIME: 30 MINUTES

COOK TIME: 20 MINUTES

SERVES: 4

GENERAL TSO'S CHICKEN

General Tso's chicken has led an interesting life. It was invented in the 1950s in Taiwan by a Hunanese chef cooking for a state banquet. He named the dish after Tso Tsung-t'ang, a famous general from Hunan. At the time, the dish reflected the flavors of the province: sour, spicy, and salty; it was not a sweet dish. It spread in popularity and eventually made its way to New York City in the 1970s, where it was sweetened with sugar for American palates. This is most likely where my dad learned about the dish. He created his own version of General Tso's, which we served in the restaurant. My brother still makes Dad's recipe at the restaurant, but he cooks it in huge batches with deep fryers. My challenge came in adapting it for home kitchens—I worked hard to honor the original flavors and textures of Dad's dish, and Eric and I taste-tested until we were satisfied. If my dad were around, I think he'd give it his stamp of approval.

FOR THE CHICKEN:

1 pound boneless skinless chicken breasts or thighs

1½ large eggs, beaten, divided

5 tablespoons cornstarch, divided

1½ tablespoons avocado oil, divided

1 teaspoon kosher salt

3 tablespoons all-purpose flour

2 teaspoons baking powder

FOR THE SAUCE:

3 tablespoons light soy sauce

3 tablespoons granulated sugar

3 tablespoons Shaoxing Chinese cooking wine

2 tablespoons ketchup

1 tablespoon oyster sauce

1 tablespoon white vinegar

1 tablespoon sweet rice vinegar

1 teaspoon dark soy sauce

½ teaspoon toasted sesame oil

¼ teaspoon hot chili paste

¼ teaspoon ground white pepper

1 • **FOR THE CHICKEN:** Cut the chicken into 2-inch chunks. In a medium bowl, combine ½ of a beaten egg, 2 tablespoons of the cornstarch, ½ tablespoon of the avocado oil, and the salt. Mix well and set aside for 15 minutes.

2 • In a medium bowl, combine the flour, the remaining 1 beaten egg, the remaining 3 tablespoons cornstarch, the baking powder, and 5 tablespoons of water. Mix until the consistency is smooth, like a runny pancake batter. Stir in the remaining 1 tablespoon of the avocado oil. Add the chicken to the batter mixture and toss to coat well.

3 • **PREPARE THE SAUCE:** In a bowl, combine the light soy sauce, sugar, cooking wine, ketchup, oyster sauce, white vinegar, rice vinegar, dark soy sauce, sesame oil, chili paste, and white pepper. Taste-test and add more sugar if you like your General Tso's chicken sweeter or if you want less heat.

(RECIPE & INGREDIENTS CONTINUE)

4 • TO COOK: Heat the oil in a large deep pot or fryer to 325°F. Another way to test the oil's temperature is to drizzle a few drops of batter into the oil. If the batter floats, the oil is hot enough. Carefully drop the chicken into the oil one piece at a time to ensure it doesn't clump together. Lower the heat as needed to prevent the oil from getting too hot and burning the chicken. Fry the chicken, flipping a few times, until light golden brown, about 4 minutes. Remove the chicken from the oil with a metal strainer. Set it aside to cool a bit on a paper towel–lined plate.

5 • Raise the temperature of the oil to 350°F and refry the chicken to make it crispier. Once golden brown, after 1 to 2 minutes, remove the chicken from the hot oil and set it aside on a paper towel–lined plate.

6 • In a medium sauté pan, add 2 to 3 tablespoons of the frying oil and heat the pan over medium-high heat.

7 • Add the dried chile peppers and cook for 15 seconds, then add the garlic, ginger, fresh chiles, and half of the scallions and cook, stirring, for 30 seconds. Add the sauce and stir for 20 more seconds. Thicken the sauce with half the cornstarch slurry, adding more if needed. Or add a little water if it becomes too thick. If desired, add the red bell pepper and the pineapple.

8 • Turn off the heat and coat the fried chicken pieces with the sauce. Serve on a large platter, and garnish the edges with broccoli and sprinkle on sesame seeds, if desired, along with the remaining scallions. Serve immediately.

COOK'S NOTE: *If you're able to, make the sauce ahead of time to allow the flavors to meld. I think it tastes even better that way.*

TO COOK:

2 cups vegetable, corn, or peanut oil

4 to 5 dried chile peppers

4 garlic cloves, minced

3 thin slices peeled ginger, minced

½ fresh red chile pepper (such as Fresno), julienned

2 scallions, white and green parts, chopped, divided

1 tablespoon cornstarch mixed with 2 tablespoons water, divided

½ red bell pepper, cored and julienned, for garnish (optional)

10 to 12 chunks canned pineapple, for garnish (optional)

Steamed broccoli crowns, for garnish (optional)

Toasted sesame seeds, for garnish (optional)

PREP TIME: 20 MINUTES

COOK TIME: 10 MINUTES

SERVES: 4

SWEET-AND-SOUR SHRIMP

Our sweet-and-sour shrimp was always a hit with customers. I'm sure it didn't hurt that my parents made sure to buy the freshest, biggest shrimp they could find. I fancy it up by butterflying the shrimp, and I make them on the crispier side by using panko breadcrumbs. Make sure to wait and add the sauce right before you're about to serve, so that the fried batter stays crispy.

FOR THE SHRIMP:

1 pound large (31/40) raw shrimp, shelled and deveined

1 tablespoon cornstarch

½ teaspoon kosher salt

¼ teaspoon ground white pepper

1 cup panko breadcrumbs

½ cup all-purpose flour

1 large egg, beaten

1 teaspoon baking powder

½ teaspoon garlic powder

3 cups vegetable, corn, or peanut oil

1 • Clean the shrimp by gently massaging them with the cornstarch and a splash of water, then rinsing off the cornstarch and draining the shrimp. Butterfly-cut the shrimp, leaving both ends attached. Season on both sides with the salt and white pepper and set aside.

2 • In a large shallow bowl, stir together the panko, flour, egg, baking powder, and garlic powder.

3 • In a wok or deep pot, heat the oil to between 280° and 300°F. Working in batches, dip the shrimp into the batter, then carefully add to the hot oil and fry until light golden brown, about 2 minutes. Place them on a paper towel–lined plate to drain the excess oil. Then refry the shrimp to make the crust crispier, an additional 15 to 30 seconds. Remove them to drain the excess oil on paper towels again and set aside.

(RECIPE & INGREDIENTS CONTINUE)

FOR THE SWEET-AND-SOUR SAUCE:

2 tablespoons vegetable oil

½ white onion, cut into 1-inch chunks

2 whole scallions, sliced into 2-inch strips

½ red bell pepper, cored and cut into 1-inch pieces

½ green bell pepper, cored and cut into 1-inch pieces

¾ cup ketchup

¾ tablespoon Shaoxing Chinese cooking wine

⅓ cup granulated sugar

¼ cup honey

⅓ cup white vinegar

1 cup canned pineapple chunks

3 tablespoons cornstarch mixed with 2 tablespoons water

4 • MAKE THE SWEET-AND-SOUR SAUCE: Heat a medium sauté pan or wok over medium-high heat and add the vegetable oil. Add the onion, scallions, and red and green bell peppers and cook, stirring constantly, to bring out the aromatics, about 2 minutes. Add the ketchup, splash the edge of the wok with the cooking wine, then add the sugar and honey and cook, stirring constantly, for 1 minute. Add 1 cup of water, the vinegar, and the pineapple and stir until the sauce appears glossy, about 1 minute. Stir in the cornstarch slurry to thicken the sauce, then remove it from the heat and pour it into a saucepan.

5 • If you're not planning to serve this dish immediately, it's best to just fry the shrimp once, set them aside, and wait to refry them until ready to serve. Reheat the sweet-and-sour sauce first and add a tablespoon of water if it has thickened a bit too much while sitting. Then heat the oil to 300°F and refry the shrimp. Pour half of the sweet-and-sour sauce on top of shrimp and serve the other half in a bowl.

6 • Serve immediately.

TSINGTAO
青島啤酒
IMPORTED
PREMIUM
LAGER

PREP TIME: 15 MINUTES

COOK TIME: 15 MINUTES

SERVES: 4

CHICKEN CHOP SUEY

- 2 boneless skinless chicken breasts, cut into 1-inch cubes
- 2 tablespoons light soy sauce, divided
- 1 tablespoon cornstarch
- 1 cup plus 1 tablespoon vegetable oil, divided
- ½ teaspoon dark mushroom soy sauce
- 2 whole scallions, sliced lengthwise
- 2 (1-inch) knobs ginger, peeled and thinly sliced
- 1 medium yellow onion, diced
- 2 medium carrots, diced
- 1 cup chopped celery
- 1 cup bean sprouts
- 1 (8-ounce) can sliced water chestnuts, drained
- 1 cup hot water or chicken broth
- 1 teaspoon granulated sugar
- 1 teaspoon kosher salt
- 2 tablespoons water mixed with 2 tablespoons cornstarch
- Cooked white rice, for serving (see page 236)
- Chinese crunchy noodles, for serving (optional)

Something I find funny about chop suey is that, as iconic as it is in the United States, I've never actually made it at home for my family. I think I always thought of it as a very Americanized version of "real" Chinese cooking. Nevertheless, it was tasty and truly what made our family restaurant survive for so many decades. In fact, even the old neon sign at our restaurant had "Chop Suey" under "Chinatown Inn." It's a super-easy meal to whip up, and, as the translation of the dish's name might indicate—it literally means "odds and ends"—you don't have to be precious with it. Feel free to swap out, omit, or add vegetables depending on what's in your fridge.

1 • In a medium bowl, rub the chicken with 1 tablespoon of the light soy sauce, the cornstarch, 1 tablespoon of the vegetable oil, and the mushroom soy sauce. Set aside.

2 • Heat a large wok over medium-high heat and add the remaining 1 cup of oil. Once hot, add the scallions and ginger. Add the chicken and cook without disturbing until seared on one side, about 2 minutes. Make sure the chicken easily comes off the wok, then flip it and cook until seared on the other side for about 2 minutes more. Stir the chicken for an additional 1 minute. Remove the chicken from the oil and set aside in a bowl.

3 • Discard all but 1 tablespoon of oil in the wok. Over medium-high heat, add the onion and cook, stirring constantly, until translucent, about 5 minutes. Add the carrots and celery and cook, stirring constantly, until tender but still crisp, about 3 minutes. Toss in the bean sprouts and water chestnuts, then stir in the hot water, the remaining tablespoon of light soy sauce, the sugar, and the salt. Add the chicken and cook, stirring constantly, for 1 minute. Bring the liquid to a boil and stir in the cornstarch slurry to thicken. Serve over rice with the crunchy noodles on top, if desired.

PREP TIME: 10 MINUTES

COOK TIME: 10 MINUTES

SERVES: 2 TO 4; MAKES 6 SMALL EGG FOO YOUNG PANCAKES

SHRIMP EGG FOO YOUNG

Egg foo young is a very popular dish and is part of our lunch combo specials at the restaurant. I never made it myself because I always thought it was too difficult, requiring a deep fryer like the big ones at the restaurant. Once I started testing it in my own kitchen for the cookbook, I figured out how to deep-fry the egg patties in my wok. I was excited to make it for my family. As one of my favorite childhood dishes, I looked forward to making it one of their favorites, too. Thank you, cookbook, for giving me the opportunity to learn something new that's old.

FOR THE SHRIMP:

10 ounces large (31/40) raw shrimp, shelled, deveined, and chopped

1 tablespoon plus 1 teaspoon cornstarch, divided

¼ teaspoon kosher salt

FOR THE GRAVY:

1 tablespoon vegetable oil

1 tablespoon all-purpose flour

½ teaspoon turmeric powder

⅛ teaspoon garlic powder

⅛ teaspoon mushroom bouillon powder

3 cups low-sodium chicken broth

2 teaspoons light soy sauce

1 tablespoon oyster sauce

½ teaspoon toasted sesame oil

¼ teaspoon ground white pepper

1 tablespoon cornstarch mixed with 2 tablespoons water

1 • Clean the chopped shrimp by massaging them with 1 tablespoon of the cornstarch and 2 tablespoons of water. Rinse the shrimp with clean, cold water. Then add the remaining 1 teaspoon of the cornstarch and the salt, toss the shrimp to coat, and set aside.

2 • **MAKE THE GRAVY:** In a medium pot or saucepan, heat the vegetable oil over medium heat. To make a roux, add the flour and cook, stirring, until it begins to become blond, about 15 seconds. Add in the turmeric, garlic powder, and bouillon powder and cook, stirring, until golden, about 15 more seconds. Slowly whisk in the chicken broth.

3 • Bring the mixture to a simmer, then stir in the soy sauce, oyster sauce, sesame oil, and white pepper. The gravy should be slightly thickened from the roux. Bring the gravy to a boil, then slowly add in the cornstarch slurry to thicken the gravy. Let cook until the gravy is glossy and thick enough to coat a spoon but still fluid, about 30 seconds. Add more slurry if needed, cover, and set aside.

(RECIPE & INGREDIENTS CONTINUE)

4 • TO CONTINUE: Heat a wok over medium-high heat and add 1 tablespoon of the oil. Toss in the seasoned shrimp and sear for 1 minute on each side. Then cook, stirring constantly, until the shrimp is pink, about 2 more minutes, taking care not to overcook. Remove the shrimp from the wok and set aside in a bowl.

5 • In a wok or deep pot over medium-high heat, heat the remaining 5 cups of the oil to 350°F. Use a thermometer to maintain the temperature. If it's too much higher than 350°F, the patties will burn; too low and the patties will separate.

6 • In a large mixing bowl, mix together the cooked shrimp, bean sprouts, and onion. Add the eggs, sesame oil, and cornstarch and lightly mix together the ingredients so that they stick together. It is important to NOT add any salt to the egg mixture, as the salt will prevent the patties from holding together.

7 • Scoop the mixture with a large soup ladle, a 2-cup measure or bowl, or a hoak (a Chinese ladle), and steadily but carefully (if you're too slow it becomes like funnel cake!) pour the mixture into the oil, using the side of the wok or pot to help create a patty in the hot oil. Keep the ladle out of the oil as much as possible—it's only used to pour the egg mixture into the oil from above. Push/float the first patty over to other side and ladle the second patty the same way. Fit only as many patties as your wok can hold or that you feel comfortable cooking at one time.

8 • Let the patties fry to golden brown on the bottom, about 30 seconds, pouring hot oil over each patty with the ladle to cook the egg faster. Then flip them to cook the opposite sides until golden, about 30 seconds. Scoop each patty with a mesh strainer and drain excess oil by gently squeezing the patty against the side of the pot, or allow it to drip on a rack.

9 • Transfer the egg foo young patties from the cooling rack to a serving plate. Heat up the gravy and pour it over top of the egg foo young. Garnish with chopped scallions and serve with rice.

TO CONTINUE:

1 tablespoon vegetable oil plus 5 cups vegetable, corn, or peanut oil, for frying, divided

2 cups white bean sprouts

½ medium yellow onion, finely chopped

6 large eggs, beaten

¼ teaspoon toasted sesame oil

1 teaspoon cornstarch

1 scallion, white and green parts, chopped, for garnish

Cooked white rice, for serving (see page 236)

PREP TIME: 15 MINUTES

COOK TIME: 10 HOURS

SERVES: 4

MAPO TOFU
WITH PORK OR TURKEY

2 tablespoons vegetable oil, divided

3 teaspoons cornstarch, divided

¾ teaspoon light soy sauce

¼ teaspoon dark mushroom soy sauce

½ pound ground meat (pork or turkey)

2 cups sliced white mushrooms

2 garlic cloves, minced

1 cup chicken broth or water

1 tablespoon doubanjiang (spicy bean paste)

1 teaspoon Shaoxing Chinese cooking wine

1 teaspoon spicy chili oil

½ teaspoon garlic powder

¼ teaspoon granulated sugar

1 whole dried Sichuan red chile

12 ounces silken firm tofu, cut into 1-inch cubes

2 teaspoons sesame oil

Cooked white rice, for serving (see page 236)

When we order takeout, nine times out of ten my husband will ask me if I want the mapo tofu. And nine times out of ten, my answer will be yes. At this point, he should stop asking and just add it to the takeout order. Mapo tofu is one of my all-time favorite comfort foods. If you've ever wondered why Chinese Americans love tofu so much, in 1800s China, meat was hard to come by, so tofu was a common protein substitute, rounding out meals.

This dish is traditionally spicy, as many Sichuan recipes can be, so adjust the heat level to your preference. This works just as well as a vegetarian dish, too—just omit the meat.

1 • In a medium nonreactive bowl, combine ½ tablespoon of the vegetable oil, 1 teaspoon of the cornstarch, the light soy sauce, and the dark mushroom soy sauce. Add the ground meat and mix well.

2 • Heat a wok over high heat and add 1 tablespoon of the vegetable oil. Brown the seasoned ground meat, breaking it up as you cook it for 6 to 8 minutes. Lower the heat to medium-high and add the mushrooms and garlic. Cook, stirring constantly, until the mushrooms have softened, about 3 minutes.

(RECIPE CONTINUES)

3 • Add the remaining ½ tablespoon of vegetable oil, the broth, doubanjiang, cooking wine, chili oil, garlic powder, sugar, and dried chile. If the mapo sauce is a bit dry, stir in ¼ cup of water. Gently add the tofu and fold the ingredients together without mashing the tofu.

4 • Add 1 tablespoon of water to the remaining 2 teaspoons of cornstarch and blend together. Bring the mapo sauce to boil and stir in the cornstarch slurry. Immediately turn off the heat.

5 • Transfer the mapo tofu to a large bowl, drizzle with the sesame oil, and serve hot with rice.

COOK'S NOTE: *In a pinch, there are pre-made mapo tofu sauces that can be added to meat and mushrooms. I've used them, and then just thrown in some of the above ingredients to make the pre-made sauce taste better.*

FEASTS FROM CHEF BABA

My stepfather, Soo Lim Yee, or Chef Baba as I'm calling him for the cookbook, had a wide-ranging repertoire when it came to the food he would cook for us, right alongside my mother, at home. Some of his American dishes we suspect came from his time in the military, cooking for troops who just wanted something hot, hearty, and familiar. Others were rooted in his upbringing in Taishan, in Guangdong province—dishes meant for celebration, comfort, or just a really satisfying Sunday night. He bridged cultures through food.

At the restaurant, he was called Boss Man (老闆). He had a commanding presence, and the staff listened to him and respected him. For me, he was just Baba (爸爸, "Dad" in Chinese). After serving in World War II, he developed a passion for cooking and took over the business from his father when he retired. I remember Baba cooking long hours in that hot kitchen, but he relished the camaraderie with the other chefs, laughing

2.

1. (previous page) Eric, me, Baba, and Mom in front of my family's Pittsburgh home. Baba passed away on October 13, 1995, just about three months after our wedding reception at the Chinatown Inn.
2. Me with my mom and dad at my Carnegie Mellon graduation. I was the first person in my family to graduate from college, a big American dream and a big moment for my parents.
3. When my parents came to visit me in New York City, I treated them to dinner at a fancy restaurant.

3.

and sharing stories and recipes. Boss Man was strict about how the food needed to be prepared, never skimping on quality or ingredients.

This chapter is full of the recipes Baba made for us at home. As kids, we never equated his cooking with love, but now I see it was his way of giving us affection. He poured his heart into every meal for us. His New England-style clam chowder was creamy and rich, with just the right amount of salt and soul. His prime rib? Always perfectly pink in the center, with a horseradish sauce that woke you right up. But his specialties were the Chinese meals he made with my mom. Whether it was steaming a whole fish with scallions and ginger, tossing beef chow fun, or making clams with black bean sauce, he was a maestro with a hot wok and spatula! It didn't matter if it was Chinese New Year or Thanksgiving—Baba's food always made meals feel like a special occasion. I remember how hungry I would get whenever he started cooking and the delicious aromas that flooded the house. It meant it was time for me to set the table for another excellent meal.

BABA'S FOOD ALWAYS MADE MEALS FEEL LIKE A SPECIAL OCCASION.

He passed down more than recipes—he passed down a legacy and nourished us with comfort food and unspoken love. So, this chapter is East meets West with a whole lot of heart. Every dish in here reminds me of his quiet strength, his sense of care, and the way food can feel like a warm hug—whether it's spicy eggplant, lobster with longevity noodles, or the best sweet potatoes you've ever had.

BABA'S CLAM CHOWDER

PREP TIME: 30 MINUTES PLUS 1 HOUR SOAK TIME

COOK TIME: 45 MINUTES

SERVES: 8

6 to 7 pounds whole fresh clams (manila or cherrystone or smaller)

5 cups boiling water

2 sticks unsalted butter, divided

1 large yellow onion, diced (about 2 cups)

1½ cups diced celery

3 cups Idaho potatoes, cut into ½-inch cubes

⅓ cup dry white wine

1 bay leaf

2 cups heavy cream

¾ cup all-purpose flour

2 teaspoons kosher salt

Freshly ground black pepper

Crusty bread, oyster crackers, or cooked white rice (see page 236), for serving (optional)

My dad often made clam chowder around the holidays as a special treat for Thanksgiving or Christmas, which elevated its status in my family. When Dad brought home clams, we always knew what that meant. I'm not exactly sure where or when he learned to make clam chowder, but he did pick up a lot of recipes while he was in the army. I like to imagine that some tough, tattooed cook taught it to him on the sly during mess hall duty.

This is a classic chowder, hearty and creamy, and serving it with crusty bread or oyster crackers makes it extra satisfying. All things being equal, though, I really like this over rice, too. You can also make the soup thicker and serve it with linguini like a clam sauce. Try it out!

1 • Rinse the clam shells, then place them in a plugged sink or in a large bowl with cold water to cover. Let the clams sit submerged for 30 minutes to allow them to "spit" out their sand. Remove the clams and discard the dirty water. Repeat the soak for another 30 minutes.

2 • Bring 5 cups of water to boil in a wok or very large pot and add the clams. Gently stir them. They should begin opening within 2 to 5 minutes. As they open, transfer them to a large bowl with a large slotted spoon. Discard the clams that remain closed. Set aside and SAVE THE WATER! This is the delicious clam juice that will be used as broth.

(RECIPE CONTINUES)

3 • Carefully pour most of the hot water into a large pot, bowl, or measuring cup. Discard the last ½ cup and any sand or dirt that has settled in the bottom of the wok. Strain the reclaimed clam water through a very-fine-mesh colander or cheesecloth to separate out any remaining dirt or sand. Another method is to let the water sit undisturbed in the bowl to allow any remaining sediment to fall to the bottom. Then just ladle the clam juice from it as you use it, leaving the last ½ cup to discard.

4 • When the clams are cool enough to handle, remove the meat from the shells. Have a small bowl handy to capture any little drops of juice to add to the clam water. Chop the clam meat into small pieces. Set aside. Discard the shells.

5 • Heat a medium stockpot over medium heat and melt 3 tablespoons of the butter. Add the onion and cook, stirring frequently, until translucent, about 7 minutes. When the onion is tender, add the celery and cook, stirring constantly, for 1 minute.

6 • Add 4 cups of the clam juice water, the potatoes, white wine, and bay leaf. Bring it to boil over high heat, then lower the heat and simmer until the potatoes are cooked through, about 25 minutes. Turn off the heat and then stir in the chopped cooked clams and the cream.

7 • In a separate small pot over medium-high heat, make a roux by melting the remaining butter and slowly adding the flour. Continuously stir the roux and cook until it is smooth but not brown, about 3 minutes. Turn the heat down slightly as needed to prevent the roux from browning.

8 • Bring the clam chowder to boil over medium-high heat and slowly stir in the roux to thicken. Stop when it's a light stew consistency, but not like a gravy or dip texture. A chowder is best when it's not too thick. Turn off the heat and stir a few times. Add the salt and continue to stir the chowder to make sure the roux is well blended and the chowder is smooth. Add black pepper to taste.

9 • Serve with your favorite crusty bread or oyster crackers—or try it over rice.

WINTER MELON SOUP

PREP TIME: 10 MINUTES

COOK TIME: 1 HOUR 15 MINUTES

SERVES: 6

2 pounds pork neck bones

3 pounds winter melon, peeled, seeded, and chopped into thick chunks

1 (3-by-1-inch) chunk of Virginia ham

1 (1-inch) knob ginger, peeled and thinly sliced

1 tablespoon dried shrimp

Kosher salt

This is a very simple soup similar to bone broth, with the shrimp and ham giving the melon a bit of extra flavor. Whether you have it before or after a meal or on its own, your body will feel nourished. Winter melon is rich in potassium, B vitamins, and vitamin C, and it promotes cardiovascular health because it is a "vasodilator," opening blood vessels and lowering your blood pressure. I actually feel more relaxed after having this soup. As I like to say, your body knows what's good for you.

1 • To a large pot, add the pork neck bones with water to cover. Over high heat, bring the water to a boil, and cook for about 10 minutes to remove impurities and blood. Discard the water and rinse the bones with cold water.

2 • Add about 5 quarts of water to a large stockpot, or enough water to cover the bones and ingredients. Add the neck bones and bring to a boil. Add the winter melon, ham, ginger, and dried shrimp. Return the water to a boil, then simmer for an additional 1 hour.

3 • Skim off the foam, add salt to taste, and serve.

COOK'S NOTE: *The meat of the neckbone is also delicious. Remove the Virginia ham if you're storing leftover soup overnight. Also, this can be made in a pressure cooker if you are pressed for time! Just be sure to skim it after cooking.*

COLD DISH
JELLYFISH

PREP TIME: 15 MINUTES PLUS OVERNIGHT MARINATING TIME

COOK TIME: 15 SECONDS

SERVES: 4 AS A SIDE DISH

Please don't let the thought of eating jellyfish scare you. It has a crunchy, fun-to-eat texture and is very refreshing, plus it's a natural source of collagen. We like to serve jellyfish at banquets as a cold-plate appetizer alongside other meats—think of it as a kind of antipasto. You won't believe how simple it is to cook, but do stay near the stove—if you cook it too long, it will shrivel up and become very tough. Give it a go!

- 8 ounces shredded, salted jellyfish
- 1 tablespoon rice vinegar
- 1 tablespoon granulated sugar
- 2 teaspoons light soy sauce
- 2 teaspoons toasted sesame oil
- ½ teaspoon kosher salt
- 2 scallions, white and green parts, chopped

1 • Rinse the salt off the jellyfish and cut it into long shreds of ¼-inch thickness. Soak the jellyfish shreds in a large bowl filled with cold water for 1 hour. Squeeze as much water out of the jellyfish as you can. Change the water in the bowl and soak the jellyfish again, overnight. Squeeze the water out of the jellyfish, then quickly rinse it in fresh water 3 more times, squeezing out the water each time.

2 • Bring a pot of water to a boil and turn off the heat. Prepare a large ice bath bowl.

3 • Swirl the jellyfish in the hot water until it's tender but still crunchy, about 15 seconds. Remove immediately and place in the ice bath. If you cook it too long, the jellyfish stiffens up and becomes tough. Squeeze the water out of the jellyfish, as much as possible.

4 • To a large mixing bowl, add the vinegar, sugar, soy sauce, sesame oil, and salt. Add the jellyfish and toss to coat. Place the bowl in the refrigerator to marinate for 1 hour or more, stirring the marinade a couple of times.

5 • Transfer the jellyfish to a plate and sprinkle with the chopped scallions.

PREP TIME: 15 MINUTES

COOK TIME: 6 MINUTES

SERVES: 4

CHICKEN AND CHINESE CELERY

For those who have never tried Chinese celery, it has a stronger flavor than standard celery, is more aromatic, and the stalks have a slightly more tender, delicate texture. You can eat all parts of it and you can cook with the leaves, so challenge yourself to use all of it. We prefer it to regular celery, but we will substitute with regular celery if we can't get it at the Chinese market. Chinese celery has many health benefits, including tons of fiber for your digestive system, so you don't have to resort to supplements if you, ahem, are having bathroom troubles.

FOR THE CHICKEN SEASONING:

2 teaspoons light soy sauce

½ teaspoon dark mushroom soy sauce

2 teaspoons vegetable oil

½ tablespoon cornstarch

1 pound chicken breast, sliced into 2-inch strips, cut on the bias

TO CONTINUE:

3 tablespoons vegetable oil, divided

2 (¼-inch-thick) slices peeled ginger (about the size of a quarter)

2 whole scallions, cut into thirds

1 bunch Chinese celery, washed, trimmed, and stalks julienned into 3-inch lengths

1 teaspoon kosher salt

1 • MAKE THE CHICKEN SEASONING: In a large bowl, combine the light soy sauce, mushroom soy sauce, vegetable oil, and cornstarch. Add the chicken and mix thoroughly.

2 • TO CONTINUE: In a large skillet or wok, heat 2 tablespoons of the vegetable oil over medium-high heat. Add the ginger, scallions, and seasoned chicken. Sear the chicken for 1 minute, then flip the pieces and sear for an additional 1 minute. Then continue cooking the chicken, stirring constantly, until cooked through, about 2 minutes. Remove from the wok and set aside on a plate.

3 • Add the remaining 1 tablespoon of oil to the wok, add the celery, and cook, stirring constantly, until crisp-tender, about 2 minutes. Add the salt, then return the chicken to the wok. Stir together well and make sure the chicken is fully cooked. Remove from the heat and serve.

COOK'S NOTE: *You can substitute American celery, but do your best to find Chinese!*

PREP TIME: 15 MINUTES PLUS 15 MINUTES MARINATING TIME

COOK TIME: 10 MINUTES

SERVES: 4

BEEF
WITH HOT GREEN PEPPERS

FOR BEEF MARINADE:

2 teaspoons light soy sauce

1 tablespoon cornstarch

1 tablespoon vegetable oil

1 (12-ounce) flank steak, cut into 2- to 3-inch julienned strips

I have another spice warning for you: Make sure to open your windows, because you will choke on the hot pepper fumes from this dish without proper ventilation. When you're julienning the pepper, make sure to wear gloves or wash your hands *really* thoroughly. Above all, do NOT touch your eyes. Now that I've hopefully scared you into compliance, I will say that the peppers calm down a bit after being cooked. So, to review, can this dish choke and blind you? Yes. Is it oh-so-satisfying? Also yes.

1 • MAKE THE MARINADE: In a large bowl, combine the soy sauce, cornstarch, and vegetable oil. Mix in the beef and set aside to marinate at room temperature for 15 minutes.

2 • TO CONTINUE: Heat a wok over high heat, add the vegetable oil, then add the ginger and scallions to flavor the oil. Add the beef and sear one side for 30 to 60 seconds, checking to make sure it's seared well. Cook the beef, stirring occasionally, searing the other side but leaving it slightly rare, about 30 seconds more. Turn off the heat and transfer the beef to a separate plate.

3 • With the remaining oil in the wok, heat over medium-high heat and add the Anaheim, serrano, and, if desired, mild peppers and the garlic. Cook, stirring constantly, for 15 to 30 seconds. You may choke a bit on the pepper fumes, so be sure to keep the hood fan on high!

4 • Drizzle the cooking wine around the sides of the wok to deglaze. Stir-fry the peppers for another 30 seconds and add the beef back to the wok. Add the light soy sauce, dark soy sauce, salt, sugar, and white pepper. Turn the heat back up to high, add the chicken broth, and cook, stirring constantly, to incorporate the flavors, about 2 minutes.

(RECIPE & INGREDIENTS CONTINUE)

5 • With the remaining liquid boiling, add the cornstarch slurry to the center of the wok and stir quickly. Immediately turn off the heat and mix well to coat entire dish. Serve with rice.

COOK'S NOTE: *The amount of serrano peppers you use will depend on how much heat you can take. The mild pepperoncini or piquillo peppers are optional, as they're mostly for color. Also, it's wise to wear some latex or food prep gloves to prevent having pepper oil on your fingers. If you accidently rub your eyes with your fingers, it will be painful.*

TO CONTINUE:

2 tablespoons vegetable oil

2 (1-inch) knobs peeled ginger

2 whole scallions, cut into thirds

5 Anaheim green peppers (mild heat), seeded and julienned into 3-inch strips

2 to 3 serrano peppers (medium to medium-high heat), seeded and julienned into 2- to 3-inch strips

2 pepperoncini or piquillo peppers (mild heat), seeded and julienned into 2- to 3-inch strips (optional; see Cook's Note)

3 garlic cloves, sliced

1 tablespoon Shaoxing Chinese cooking wine

1 tablespoon light soy sauce

1 teaspoon dark soy sauce

½ teaspoon kosher salt

½ teaspoon granulated sugar

⅛ teaspoon ground white pepper

¼ cup chicken broth

½ tablespoon cornstarch mixed with 1 tablespoon of water

Cooked white rice, for serving (see page 236)

PREP TIME: 20 MINUTES

COOK TIME: 20 MINUTES

SERVES: 4

CHICKEN CHOW MEIN

1 pound boneless skinless chicken breast, cut into 1-inch cubes

2 teaspoons light soy sauce

½ teaspoon dark mushroom soy sauce

2 tablespoons plus 2 teaspoons vegetable oil, divided

½ tablespoon cornstarch

2 whole scallions, 1 cut into thirds, 1 chopped, divided

1 (¼-inch-thick) slice peeled ginger (about the size of a quarter)

½ yellow onion, thinly sliced

1 cup broccoli florets

1 cup chopped bok choy

1 carrot, peeled and cut thinly on the bias or into strips

4 white mushrooms, sliced

2 garlic cloves, minced

½ cup chicken broth, divided

2 teaspoons kosher salt

⅛ teaspoon ground white pepper

1 (1-pound) package of fresh Chinese egg noodles (chow mein)

"Chow mein" is a Cantonese phrase that roughly translates to "stir-fried noodles." It's a necessity in our pantry, sort of like our version of spaghetti. I always try to keep chow mein noodles stocked in the house. Try chow mein with spicy chili oil or any hot sauce, like I do, for that extra kick.

1 • In a large bowl, mix the chicken breast cubes with the light soy sauce, mushroom soy sauce, 2 teaspoons of the vegetable oil, and the cornstarch.

2 • In a large wok over high heat, add 1 tablespoon of the oil. Add the scallion that is cut into thirds and the ginger, then push them to the side and add the chicken. Let the chicken sear on one side for about 1 minute. Flip the pieces and sear the chicken on the other side for 1 minute, then cook through, stirring constantly, for 2 more minutes. Remove the chicken from the wok and set aside.

3 • Add the remaining 1 tablespoon of oil to the wok and turn the heat down to medium-high. Add the onion and cook, stirring constantly, for 1 minute, then add the broccoli, bok choy, carrot, mushrooms, and garlic. Add a splash of the chicken broth and cook, stirring constantly, for 2 minutes. Season with the salt and white pepper. Add the egg noodles and stir to warm through.

4 • Stir in the chicken and the remaining chicken broth. Make sure chicken is cooked through. Add more salt and pepper to taste, if desired.

5 • Transfer the chicken and vegetables to a serving plate and garnish with the chopped scallions.

CHOW FUN

NOODLES WITH BEEF

PREP TIME: 15 MINUTES

COOK TIME: 10 MINUTES

SERVES: 4

This dish is great if you're gluten-free or gluten intolerant because it uses rice noodles. I find rice noodles to be superior to other kinds of gluten-free pasta because the noodles have a nice bite to them. Don't do yourself a disservice by using dry noodles—try your best to find them fresh at an Asian market. You'll thank me later.

FOR THE BEEF MARINADE:

1 (8-ounce) flank steak

2 teaspoons vegetable oil

2 teaspoons cornstarch

1 teaspoon light soy sauce

½ teaspoon dark mushroom soy sauce

FOR THE NOODLES:

12 ounces fresh wide rice noodles

4 tablespoons vegetable oil, divided

3 whole scallions, cut into thirds

2 (1-inch) knobs ginger, peeled, divided

2 tablespoons Shaoxing Chinese cooking wine

½ teaspoon sesame oil

1 tablespoon light soy sauce

2 teaspoons dark mushroom soy sauce

¼ teaspoon granulated sugar

½ teaspoon kosher salt

¼ teaspoon ground white pepper

6 ounces fresh mung bean sprouts

1 • **MAKE THE BEEF MARINADE:** Slightly freeze the flank steak to make slicing easier, then slice the meat into very thin pieces. In a bowl, mix the beef with the vegetable oil, cornstarch, light soy sauce, and mushroom soy sauce and let sit for 15 minutes, covered, on the counter.

2 • **MAKE THE NOODLES:** Fresh rice noodles can be very stiff and stuck together. Prepare a large bowl of warm water and spin the noodles around in the bowl to loosen them up for 30 seconds, then drain well. Set aside.

3 • Heat a wok over high heat, then add 2 tablespoons of the oil to coat the wok. Add 3 pieces of scallion and 1 piece of ginger to flavor the oil, then add the marinated beef. Sear the beef on one side for 30 to 60 seconds, then cook, stirring occasionally, to sear the other side, about 30 seconds more. Remove from the wok and set aside.

(RECIPE CONTINUES)

4 • Lower the heat to medium, add the remaining 2 tablespoons of the oil to the wok, and add the remaining scallions and ginger. Spread the rice noodles evenly across the wok and cook quickly, stirring constantly, for 15 seconds. Drizzle the cooking wine around the sides of the wok to deglaze. Continue to stir the noodles to prevent them from sticking. Add the sesame oil, light soy sauce, mushroom soy sauce, sugar, and cooked beef. Season with the salt and white pepper. Finally, toss in the bean sprouts and cook, stirring constantly, until evenly coated and the sprouts are tender.

5 • Serve hot.

COOK'S NOTE: *Here's a trick: If you want the meat to be more tender, you can add ¼ teaspoon of baking soda to the marinade. I find it changes the texture of the meat and makes it too mushy if left for longer than 15 minutes, although some people like a fattier-feeling texture.*

PRIME RIB

PREP TIME: 15 MINUTES
PLUS 4 HOURS 30 MINUTES
MARINATING AND RESTING TIME

COOK TIME: 2 HOURS 20 MINUTES

SERVES: 4 TO 6

FOR THE PRIME RIB:

1 (4-pound) boneless prime rib roast

2 teaspoons kosher salt

3 tablespoons vegetable oil

FOR THE MARINADE:

⅓ cup light soy sauce

4 garlic cloves, chopped

3 whole scallions, chopped

2 fresh red chile peppers (such as Fresno), sliced

1 tablespoon honey

1 tablespoon toasted sesame oil

2 teaspoons kosher salt

My dad was a big meat man. He'd often come home late from the restaurant, not having eaten yet (ironic, right?), and head to the kitchen for some steak. For him, it was a quick, satisfying meal. New York strip, T-bone, ribeye—he'd eat it all. My brother and I would wake up to the tantalizing smell of steak searing and escape our beds to beg him to share. As delicious as those late-night steaks were, Dad reserved prime rib for special occasions, like birthdays or family visits. He always nailed it, cooking the prime rib to a perfect medium rare. I've since taken up the tradition, making prime rib on holidays, hoping to get my steak as tender and juicy as Dad's was.

1 • Sprinkle the prime rib with the salt, then refrigerate it in a very large bowl for 3 hours.

2 • **MAKE THE MARINADE:** In a bowl, combine the soy sauce, garlic, scallions, chiles, honey, sesame oil, and salt. Retrieve the prime rib from the refrigerator and pour the marinade over the beef. Allow it to sit out to reach close to room temperature before cooking, 1 to 2 hours.

3 • **MEANWHILE, PREPARE THE AU JUS:** Heat a large stockpot or enamel pot over medium-high heat and add the oil. Add the neckbone or shank bone and sear all sides of the meat, about 5 minutes.

4 • Add the onion and cook, stirring constantly, until translucent, about 6 minutes. Add half of the beef stock, plus the celery, carrots, and garlic. Bring it to a boil and add the red wine and tomato paste. Add the remaining beef broth, thyme, and bay leaves and stir to combine. Bring it to a boil, then lower the temperature to a simmer and cook for 30 minutes.

(RECIPE & INGREDIENTS CONTINUE)

5 • Remove the shank bone, then strain out everything, leaving just the au jus. You can save the solids, including the vegetables, to make a stew or flavor another dish.

6 • Preheat the oven to 250°F.

7 • Remove as much of marinade from the prime rib as possible, dabbing it dry with paper towels. Heat a large skillet over medium-high heat and add the oil. Sear all sides of the prime rib, 5 to 7 minutes.

8 • Place the prime rib on a roasting rack and roast in the oven for 1 hour and 40 minutes to achieve medium rare. Remove the prime rib and tent it with tin foil for 30 minutes to rest.

9 • Slice the prime rib ½ inch thick and serve drizzled with au jus and salt and pepper to taste.

FOR THE AU JUS:

2 tablespoons vegetable oil

2 pounds neckbone or shank bone

½ medium yellow onion, chopped

1 (32-ounce) box beef stock, divided

3 celery stalks, cut into 3-inch pieces

2 medium carrots, cut into 3-inch pieces

5 garlic cloves, sliced

½ cup dry red wine

1 tablespoon tomato paste

2 fresh thyme sprigs

2 bay leaves

PREP TIME: 15 MINUTES

COOK TIME: 20 MINUTES

SERVES: 4

CLAMS
WITH BLACK BEANS AND GARLIC

2 pounds fresh manila clams

1 tablespoon oyster sauce

2 teaspoons light soy sauce

1 teaspoon dark mushroom soy sauce

⅛ teaspoon ground white pepper

2 teaspoons granulated sugar

1 tablespoon vegetable oil

3 garlic cloves, minced

1 (1-inch) knob ginger, peeled and minced

½ yellow onion, diced

2 scallions, white and green parts, chopped

2 fresh red chile peppers (such as Fresno), seeded and cored, finely chopped

This dish is so intensely flavorful—you get the brine from the clams, the heat from the peppers, and the umami from the fermented black beans (don't skip this ingredient!). I use manila clams because they're small and sweet, but you can certainly use other varieties. Just make sure you give your clams enough time to sit in water—grit is the last thing you want on your plate or in your mouth.

1 • Rinse the clams in cold water, then fill a sink or large bowl with enough cold water to completely cover them. Let the clams sit for 30 to 60 minutes to spit out the sand.

2 • Boil 5 cups of water in a large stockpot or wok. Add the clams and blanch until they open, 2 to 5 minutes. Immediately remove the clams that pop open with a large slotted spoon and set them aside in a bowl. Discard any unopened clams.

3 • Carefully pour the hot water, now known as clam juice, into a large bowl. Set aside.

4 • In another bowl, stir together the oyster sauce, light soy sauce, mushroom soy sauce, white pepper, and sugar. Ladle 1 cup of the clam juice into the sauce. Set aside.

(RECIPE & INGREDIENTS CONTINUE)

½ medium green bell pepper, cored and diced

½ medium red bell pepper, cored and diced

2 tablespoons black bean and garlic sauce

2 teaspoons fermented black beans, rinsed and drained (optional)

1 tablespoon Shaoxing Chinese cooking wine

2 teaspoons cornstarch mixed with 2 tablespoons water

Cooked white rice, for serving (see page 236)

5 • Wipe the wok clean and dry with paper towels. Heat the wok over medium heat and add the vegetable oil. Add the garlic and ginger and cook, stirring constantly, for 30 seconds, then add the onion, scallions, and chile peppers. Lower the heat to prevent the garlic from burning and cook, stirring constantly, for 1 minute. Add the green and red bell peppers, black bean and garlic sauce, and fermented black beans, if desired. Add the clam sauce and cook, stirring constantly, for 1 minute. Add the cooked clams and the cooking wine and gently blend the sauce with the clams.

6 • Once the sauce comes to a boil, drizzle in some of the cornstarch slurry and thicken the sauce until it is a glossy gravy. You don't have to use up all the slurry. If the sauce becomes too thick, add ½ cup of clam juice to thin.

7 • Transfer to a serving dish and serve immediately with rice.

退休
A12
香

PREP TIME: 20 MINUTES

COOK TIME: 10 MINUTES

SERVES: 4

SALT-AND-PEPPER SHRIMP

1 pound large (31/35) shrimp with shells, deveined, legs removed

1 tablespoon garlic salt

¼ teaspoon ground white pepper

⅛ teaspoon kosher salt

1 cup vegetable oil

2 garlic cloves, minced

½ red onion, diced

2 whole scallions, chopped, divided

1 small Thai green chile, thinly sliced into rounds

Peel-and-eat shrimp are so fun to eat, don't you think? And leaving the shells on adds so much flavor. Sometimes we even eat the shells because they are so delicious when fried, like shrimp chips—and hey, the shell is probably good for you. It's got calcium!

1 • Cut a slit in the back of the shrimp shells from head to tail. Pat the shrimp dry with paper towels or a kitchen towel.

2 • In a small bowl, make a dry mix by combing the garlic salt, white pepper, and salt. Set aside.

3 • In a large wok, heat the vegetable oil to 375°F. Fry the shrimp in batches so that the oil covers the shrimp but they're not overcrowded. Remove the shrimp using a metal strainer once they turn orange, about 45 seconds. Place the shrimp on paper towels to absorb excess oil. Once all the shrimp is fried, let the oil cool a bit, then strain it into a tempered glass measuring cup. Reuse this oil to cook the remaining ingredients.

4 • Wipe the wok clean using paper towels. Heat 1 tablespoon of the reserved oil over medium heat. First add the minced garlic, then add the onion, ⅓ of the scallions, and the chile and cook, stirring, until aromatic, about 1 minute. Add the shrimp back in and mix together.

5 • Sprinkle the dry mix of garlic salt, white pepper, and salt over the shrimp a little bit at a time, and toss the shrimp to coat evenly. Serve topped with the remaining chopped scallions.

PREP TIME: 40 MINUTES

COOK TIME: 10 MINUTES

SERVES: 4

HONG KONG LOBSTER
WITH LONG-LIFE NOODLES

Talk about a full-circle moment. I remember having this dish a few years ago at a Chinese restaurant in Arcadia, California, and it brought me back to Hong Kong. Long-life noodles, also known as yi mein, signify longevity because the noodles are long, just as we hope our lives will be. We always serve long-life noodles at Chinese New Year or on someone's birthday to wish them good health. These noodles are fried before they're packaged so they have an interesting, springy texture once boiled. I can't promise that if you eat this you'll magically extend your life, but I *can* guarantee that you'll have an amazingly flavorful meal worthy of celebrating.

2 whole (1½-pound) live lobsters (optional but not as tasty is to use 3 fresh or frozen lobster tails)

FOR THE LOBSTER SAUCE:

1 tablespoon Shaoxing Chinese cooking wine

1 tablespoon light soy sauce

1 tablespoon oyster sauce

1 teaspoon granulated sugar

½ teaspoon kosher salt

¼ teaspoon ground white pepper

FOR THE NOODLES:

14 ounces yi mein (fried noodles)

1 tablespoon vegetable oil

2 scallions, white and green parts separated, cut into 2- to 3-inch pieces

1 garlic clove, minced

1 tablespoon oyster sauce

1½ teaspoons light soy sauce

⅛ teaspoon ground white pepper

1 • Place the live lobsters in the freezer for 5 to 10 minutes.

2 • **MAKE THE LOBSTER SAUCE:** In a small bowl, combine the cooking wine, light soy sauce, oyster sauce, sugar, salt, and white pepper. Set aside.

3 • **MAKE THE NOODLES:** Bring 6 cups of water to a boil in a large wok. Add the yi mien noodles and separate them with chopsticks or tongs. Keep stirring and moving the noodles to fluff and separate. Boil for 2 to 3 minutes, then test the noodles to see if the middles are just slightly spongy, taking care not to overcook them. Turn off the heat. Set ½ cup of the noodle cooking water aside to use later and transfer the noodles to a large bowl. Rinse them to stop further cooking. Drain.

4 • Empty the remaining hot water from the wok and wipe it dry. Heat the wok over medium-high heat for 30 seconds, then add the vegetable oil. Add the white parts of the scallions and the garlic, then return the noodles to the wok. Add the oyster sauce, soy sauce, and white pepper and mix well, making sure the noodles are not sticking together. If they seem dry, add some of the reserved noodle water. Add the green parts of the scallions and cook, stirring, for 30 seconds. Transfer the noodles to a large platter.

(RECIPE & INGREDIENTS CONTINUE)

FOR THE LOBSTERS:

5 tablespoons cornstarch

2 cups vegetable, corn, or peanut oil

4 scallions, white parts julienned, green parts cut in 2- to 3-inch pieces, divided

7 (¼-inch) slices of ginger with skin, washed and dried

5 garlic cloves, smashed, peeled, and roughly chopped

1 tablespoon Shaoxing Chinese cooking wine

2 tablespoons cornstarch mixed with 2 tablespoons water

½ teaspoon toasted sesame oil

5 • PREP THE LOBSTERS: Remove the lobsters from the freezer—freezing should make them more lethargic as the cold desensitizes them. Place 1 lobster on a large cutting board, belly-side down. To humanely kill it, use a sharp chef's knife and place the tip of the knife on top of the lobster's head, slightly behind the eyes. Push the knife straight down in one motion. It may still move in parts, but it will be dead.

6 • Grab the head shell and pull and twist to separate it from the tail. There will be some greenish "mustard" inside the exposed head. Some people like the umami flavor of this part and will cook it with the lobster or in another dish. For this recipe, we will discard it.

7 • Cut both of the front claws from the body with a clean chop of the cleaver by slicing off the front part of the head. This should remove both claws as well as the mouth of the lobster in one go. Discard the mouth section and keep the claws.

8 • The fuzzy gills on either side of the lobster are inedible. Push the gills away from the sides of the body and slice them and the legs off with the cleaver. Separate the gills from the legs. Discard the gills and keep the legs.

9 • Cut the remaining body and the tail in half lengthwise. Clean out the dark strip of "mustard" and the occasional roe found along the bottom half of the tail. Make sure to remove any sand tracks that may remain. Throw out the dark strip and sand tracks. Chop the head sections and the tail into 4 equal parts.

10 • Remove the rubber bands from the claws. Lay the claws light side up for easier chopping. Chop the elbow away from the claw and cut it in half or smash it with a mallet or cleaver to crack the shell. Then chop the claw part in half between the pinchers. Clean out and discard everything that remains inside the head pieces. Repeat with the other lobster.

11 • In a large colander, rinse all the pieces with water, removing and discarding any small bits of the shell. Lay the lobster out on some paper towels to dry further. Keep the legs separate from the rest, as they will be cooked last.

12 • Coat any exposed lobster meat with the cornstarch—this will help to seal the juices in when flash frying and cooking. The shell does not need to be coated with the cornstarch, but it's okay if some gets on the shell.

13 • In a small saucepan over medium-high heat, bring 2¼ cups of water to a boil.

14 • Make sure the wok is completely dry. Heat the wok over high heat and add the cooking oil. Carefully but as quickly as possible, add one piece of lobster at a time, sliding it down the side of the wok into the oil to prevent too much oil from splashing. If you have only a small wok, cook the lobster in small batches. The lobster cooks very quickly—as soon as the shell turns red and the meat is white but still slightly translucent, remove the lobster with a wok spatula to a flat strainer over the wok. Then place the cooked lobster in a bowl or metal tray. Continue cooking the lobster until all pieces but the legs are cooked, monitoring and reducing the heat if it gets too hot. Turn off the heat. This oil is now flavored with lobster. Transfer this oil carefully into a small pot, leaving about 2 tablespoons in the wok.

15 • Turn the heat back up to high. Add the white parts of the scallions, ginger, and garlic and cook, stirring constantly, for about 20 seconds. Toss in the flash-fried lobster and the uncooked legs and stir-fry for 30 seconds. Add the cooking wine and 2 cups of the boiling water, then add the reserved lobster sauce mixture. Cover for 30 to 45 seconds, then remove the lid and add the cornstarch slurry to thicken the sauce.

16 • Add the remaining green parts of the scallions, 1 tablespoon of the reserved lobster-flavored oil, and the sesame oil and cook, stirring constantly, for 15 seconds.

17 • Serve the lobster on the noodles and cover it with the sauce from the wok.

COOK'S NOTE: *Cutting a live lobster requires effort and knowledge. It is also not for the faint of heart, as the lobster's nervous system continues to move and twitch its parts even after it's been killed. For those who prefer not to go through this process, use lobster tails instead. Or have the seafood man cut it up for you and put it in an ice box. Keep it refrigerated until ready to cook. It should be cooked immediately for the best flavor.*

STEAMED FISH
WITH SCALLIONS AND GINGER

PREP TIME: 10 MINUTES

COOK TIME: 10 MINUTES

SERVES: 4

4 frozen tilapia fillets (about 1 pound total)

1 (3-inch) knob ginger, peeled and thinly sliced

⅛ teaspoon kosher salt

2 scallions, white and green parts, julienned

¼ cup vegetable oil

3 tablespoons light soy sauce

Cooked white rice, for serving (see page 236)

As a kid, I remember my mother meticulously cleaning and scaling whole fish whenever she'd cook this dish. She'd actually cook two fish, then freeze one for leftovers because it was so much prep work—it usually took her an hour, and that was before she even started cooking. I admire the fact that Mom was so committed to cooking this dish authentically, but I don't have time for that, and I'm going to guess you don't either. Instead of whole fish, I use frozen fillets, and it's so much easier—plus you don't have to eat around the bones. Make sure you have enough rice, because the sauce over rice is heaven! I love it so much that even if all the fish is gone, I'll pour any remaining sauce into a small glass bowl, refrigerate it, and heat it up to have with rice the next day.

1 • Set up a large steamer using a heatproof rack, trivet, or steamer insert in a large pot with a tight-fitting lid. Add water to the pot until it reaches just below the rack's surface, usually 1 to 2 inches deep.

2 • Defrost the fish, rinse, and pat dry with paper towels. Place the fillets on a heatproof platter that can fit inside your steamer. Add the sliced ginger and spread it evenly over each fillet.

3 • Over medium-high heat, bring the water in the pot to a boil. Carefully place the plate with the fish in the steamer. Cover and steam, maintaining a simmer, for 7 minutes. Check that the fish is done by gently lifting the meat. If it sticks, then cook for another minute. When the meat lifts easily, then it is done.

4 • Remove the fish and plate from the steamer, draining any water that accumulates on the plate (carefully—it's hot!). You can serve the fish from this plate or transfer it to a serving platter. Sprinkle the fish evenly with the salt. Add the julienned scallion on top to garnish.

5 • Heat the vegetable oil in a small saucepan over medium-high heat until you see the first sign of "steam"; that's when you'll know it's hot enough. Drizzle the soy sauce over the fish and then pour the hot oil over the fish and the scallions. Serve with rice.

CHINESE SPICY EGGPLANT

PREP TIME: 40 MINUTES

COOK TIME: 15 MINUTES

SERVES: 4

I know eggplant can be divisive, but I really want you to give this a try if you're in the "No, thank you!" camp. Just make sure to buy Asian eggplants rather than the much larger Mediterranean ones—Asian eggplants are longer and thinner and the texture is much less spongy. Another handy tip to have in your back pocket: how to keep the beautiful purple vibrancy of the eggplant. I was always a little rueful when cooking the eggplant dulled its color—that is, until a professional chef let me in on an amazing secret. If you soak the eggplant in some vinegar, it'll magically keep its color! This step isn't necessary, but the dish really is more visually striking if you do it.

FOR THE EGGPLANT:

3 Chinese or Asian eggplants

3 tablespoons white vinegar

FOR THE SAUCE:

3 tablespoons brown sugar or granulated sugar

2 tablespoons light soy sauce

2 teaspoons dark soy sauce

2 tablespoons oyster sauce

2 tablespoons white vinegar

1 tablespoon Shaoxing Chinese cooking wine

2 teaspoons cornstarch

1 teaspoon doubanjiang (spicy bean paste)

1 • MAKE THE EGGPLANT: Set up a large steamer using a heatproof rack, trivet, or steamer insert in a large pot with a tight-fitting lid. Add water to the pot until it reaches just below the rack's surface, usually 1 to 2 inches deep.

2 • Wash and slice the eggplant horizontally (crosswise) every 2 inches, then slice those pieces lengthwise in half and then again lengthwise so that they are 2-inch-long by ½-inch-wide batons. Place them in a heatproof bowl that can fit in the steamer. The part closest to the stem needs longer to cook because it's tougher, so put those pieces in last, on top, cut side facing up. Drizzle the white vinegar over the eggplant and turn the pieces over a few times until coated, then add water just to cover the eggplant. Set aside for 10 minutes.

3 • Over medium-high heat, bring the water in the pot to a boil. Drain the water from the bowl with the eggplant and place the bowl in the steamer. Cover the pot. Maintain a steady simmer and steam the eggplant until soft but not mushy, about 15 minutes, adding more water if needed. Remove the eggplant from the steamer.

(RECIPE & INGREDIENTS CONTINUE)

4 • MAKE THE SAUCE: In a bowl, mix together the sugar, light and dark soy sauces, oyster sauce, vinegar, cooking wine, cornstarch, spicy bean paste, and ¼ cup water. Taste to see if the sauce is to your liking and adjust as needed. Set aside.

5 • TO CONTINUE: Heat a wok over medium-high heat and add 2 tablespoons of the oil. Add the fresh and dried chile peppers and cook, stirring constantly, for 30 seconds. Add the garlic and ginger and cook, stirring, for another 30 seconds. Add the remaining tablespoon of oil, the mushrooms (if desired), and half the scallions and cook, stirring constantly, for another minute.

6 • Add the sauce and stir until the sauce boils. Add the steamed eggplant and mix with the sauce for 2 minutes to coat well. Then stir in the sesame oil.

7 • Serve with rice and a scallion garnish!

COOK'S NOTE: *If you'd prefer not to steam, another option is to soak the cut eggplant in salted water for 30 minutes. Drain, then toss with 2 tablespoons of cornstarch to coat and stir-fry in oil until tender.*

TO CONTINUE:

3 tablespoons vegetable oil, divided

1 fresh red chile pepper (such as Fresno), sliced

2 dried red chiles

4 garlic cloves, minced

3 thin slices peeled ginger, minced

1 cup sliced fresh shiitake mushrooms (optional)

2 scallions, white and green parts, chopped, divided

1 teaspoon toasted sesame oil

Cooked white rice, for serving (see page 236)

PREP TIME: 5 MINUTES

COOK TIME: 50 MINUTES

SERVES: 4 AS A SIDE DISH

YUMMY SWEET POTATOES

- 4 medium sweet potatoes
- ½ cup packed dark brown sugar
- 3 tablespoons unsalted butter, thinly sliced
- 1 tablespoon granulated sugar
- ⅛ teaspoon ground cinnamon

I can't say definitively where my dad picked up this recipe, but I'm going to guess it was during his time as a cook in World War II. He learned to make a lot of American dishes then—he was a foodie who loved learning from the other cooks during an otherwise grim time. The Chinese generally roast sweet potatoes and eat them plain—which is perfectly good, don't get me wrong. But I have a sweet tooth, so adding brown sugar (and butter—don't forget the butter!) felt like a luxury to me the first time my dad served me these. I now can't have them any other way during Thanksgiving or, really, any time I'm in the mood. Seriously, these are tasty year-round, so don't be afraid to make them on a random weekday!

1 • Place whole potatoes in a large pot and fill it with enough water to cover by an inch. Bring the water to a boil and cook the sweet potatoes until tender but still firm, about 30 minutes. Drain and cool the potatoes in cold water until you're able to handle them.

2 • Preheat the oven to 400°F.

3 • Gently peel away the potato skins. They should come off very easily. Cut the potatoes horizontally into halves or thirds depending on how long each is. You want about a 3-inch length for each section. Then cut those sections in half and cut the halves into wedges.

4 • Line a sheet pan with aluminum foil. Place the cut potatoes in neat rows with their wedge sides up, if possible. Sprinkle the tops with dark brown sugar. Add the butter slices on top, then sprinkle the granulated sugar and cinnamon over everything.

(RECIPE CONTINUES)

5 • Place the sheet pan on the middle rack and bake the potatoes for 10 minutes. Test a piece of potato to be sure it's cooked through but still retains firmness (no mushy candied sweet potatoes, please!). With a baking brush, brush the melted liquid from the bottom of the pan over all the sweet potatoes.

6 • Move the baking sheet to an upper rack of the oven and turn the temperature to broil. Broil the potatoes for 10 minutes to char some of the edges. Since every oven is different, keep an eye on the potatoes to make sure they don't burn too much. You're looking for a slight crunch from the char.

7 • Remove and try not to eat all of these before dinner is ready. Believe me, you won't be able to resist them . . . especially when they're hot. I've found that one way to prevent this from happening is to bake the potatoes, then take them out and set them aside, waiting until the first course is almost done to do the broiling part.

COOK'S NOTE: *To keep the brown sugar from getting hard, fill a teabag pouch with some uncooked rice and secure it with string. Place the teabag in the sugar in an airtight container.*

BABY SNOW PEA LEAVES

PREP TIME: 10 MINUTES

COOK TIME: 5 MINUTES

SERVES: 4 AS A SIDE DISH

Large bundle of snow pea leaves (usually comes in 1-pound bags)

3 tablespoons vegetable oil

4 garlic cloves, cut in slivers

½ tablespoon Shaoxing Chinese cooking wine

1 teaspoon kosher salt

There was a time when snow pea leaves were strictly seasonal, which made them a special item to serve. But these days it seems you can find them any time of year. We eat snow pea leaves (and yes, even these are sometimes called "Chinese broccoli"!) as a side dish. As I've mentioned, we don't eat raw vegetables, and we don't do salads. We cook all our vegetables, so this is our way to get greens on the table. My mom loves to eat this, but she is very particular about picking through the leaves (which is a lot of work!), so she doesn't love to make them. In my opinion, you don't need to be quite so fastidious with the leaves. You need a big bundle of leaves because they shrink, much like spinach cooks way down. But they're so delicious, tender, and sweet.

1 • Soak the snow pea leaves in cold water to remove any dirt. Rinse them further in a colander, then dry the leaves in a salad spinner or with a kitchen towel. Remove the tendrils and little flowers and stems that seem tough, dry, or old, and remove any browning or yellow leaves.

2 • Heat a large skillet or wok over medium-high, then add the vegetable oil. Add the garlic slivers and cook, stirring constantly to flavor the oil, for a few seconds. Add the snow pea leaves, then drizzle the cooking wine around the sides of the wok or skillet. Cook, stirring constantly, until the leaves turn bright green, about 3 minutes. Add the salt.

3 • Transfer the snow pea leaves to a serving plate. Any remaining water in the wok should not be added to the dish.

COOK'S NOTE: *A Baby Snow Pea Tutorial: What to look for when choosing snow pea leaves? Avoid bright-green leaves with little tendrils or flowers, as those indicate that the stems may be tough. The snow peas would still be edible, but it's more work to pluck the leaves away from the stems. The way to tell if the stems are tender and crisp is by feel. Or you can boil one stalk to make sure the stems are not tough and chewy. If the stems are tough, it's best to just remove the leaves from the stems, discard the stems, and just use leaves—in which case, adjust the recipe to 3 garlic cloves, 1 teaspoon cooking wine, and ½ teaspoon salt.*

MING-NA'S KITCHEN

I recently renovated our kitchen to create my DREAM kitchen. It is not just big and beautiful but super functional and practical. It is my sanctuary and happy place. Now, I've had many kitchens in my lifetime and have spent countless hours making food for myself, friends, and family. I have cooked in everything from a tiny New York City kitchen tucked in a studio apartment to a 1920s Spanish-style kitchen when I first moved to Los Angeles to the sleek modern kitchen I had while filming in Vancouver. I even set up a full working kitchen in my garage during our renovation and cooked in there for more than six months! This is how much I love and need to cook.

Having gained experience in so many types of kitchens, I knew exactly what I wanted and needed in my dream kitchen. I personally designed every drawer, chose every appliance, and figured out what worked best for me. My favorite thing to do is pin my hair up into a messy bun, turn up the flame on my wok burner (with 35,000 BTU; yes, I'm bragging about this), and cook up a meal for the family. This is where the magic

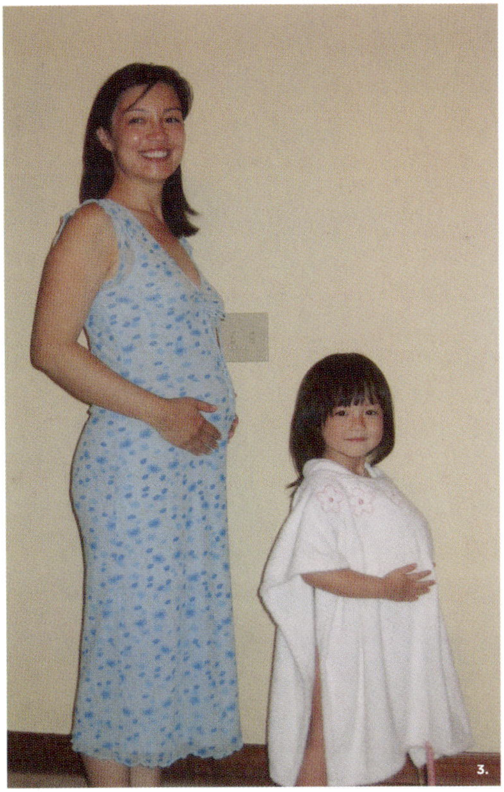

1. My mother and me at my Carnegie Mellon graduation. She was very proud of my high honor cords—a good Asian daughter! My drama degree launched me into my acting career.
2. A Maui elopement. June 16, 1995.
3. Me and Michaela, both showing.
4. Eric, Michaela, me, and baby Cooper.

(and oftentimes the chaos) happens. I may have a fabulous new kitchen, but I am still a very messy cook. And proud of it! If you are one, too, I want you to celebrate your artistic flair in the kitchen!

This is a collection of the recipes I've made my own over the years. Some are cozy, nostalgic Chinese comfort dishes, like congee or lion's head meatballs. Others are dishes I fell in love with at restaurants and just *had* to figure out how to make at home—yes, I am that person who asks the waiter, "So . . . what's in the sauce?" and then goes full food-detective mode until I've cracked it. These recipes are a mix of family favorites, late-night cravings, and experiments that turned out so deliciously I had to actually write them down. (Looking at you, Slobby Joes with Onion Rings (page 191)!) Normally when I cook, I eyeball ingredient measurements or go by feel, smell, and taste. Working on this cookbook, I had to measure out every ingredient. There were many days when I felt like a mad scientist with all my measuring cups and spoons splayed out all over the kitchen counter. It was tedious and hard work, but I became obsessed with making sure I got the recipes right. It was important to me because it's a reflection of who I am. I want to share what I eat and have these dishes represent with complete authenticity how I live—a little Chinese, a little American, a little international, with a whole lot of fun and love. But more than that, this chapter is about self-discovery—of learning who I am through food. Going from a struggling actress fresh out of college to a wife and then a mother of two beautiful children, cooking helped me to grow as a person. It grounds me and keeps me connected to the people I love.

I've been lucky enough to live, travel, and work all over the world, and those experiences have also found their way into my home cooking. And like my mom and Baba, I learned there is nothing more joyful than sharing my cooking with loved ones. Whether it's Pesto Salmon (page 193), Hubby's Chinese Chicken Wings (page 183), or French Vietnamese Black Pepper Steak (page 215), each dish carries a memory, a story, or a spark of flavor from a place that left an impression on me. I hope these recipes will create positive memories for you and your loved ones, as they have for my kids, family, and friends. This chapter is not just about feeding the people I love—it's about honoring where I come from, where I've been, and the beautiful in-between. And I hope that, somewhere in here, you find something that feels like home to you, too.

PREP TIME: 15 MINUTES

COOK TIME: 5 MINUTES PER CREPE

SERVES: 4

CREPES WITH NUTELLA

- 2 large eggs plus 1 egg white, at room temperature
- 1 cup whole milk, at room temperature
- 6 tablespoons unsalted butter, divided
- 1 cup all-purpose flour
- ¼ cup water, at room temperature
- 1 tablespoon granulated sugar
- 1 teaspoon pure vanilla extract
- ¼ teaspoon kosher salt
- 2 tablespoons Nutella

Crepes with Nutella always transport me back to our very first family trip to Paris. Eric, the kids, and I loved to amble down Rue de Montparnasse, studying the crepe stands that dotted the street until we found one we all agreed had particularly tasty-looking crepes. The crepe maker poured batter onto the hot griddle and expertly twisted his "rozell" (batter spreader) in circles to spread the batter and shape the crepe. He then filled the crepe with Nutella, which immediately started melting, so you had to eat it quickly! Heaven on Earth.

I returned from Paris determined to master crepe making so I could make them for the kids. After a few less-than-perfect attempts, I got the technique down. Don't be scared! I promise you can do it, too, if you practice. Just know that your first crepe always comes out wonky. Think of this as your opportunity to be a very elevated short-order cook for your loved ones. Oh, and of course it's also an opportunity to eat Nutella for breakfast. Win-win!

1 • Immerse the eggs in lukewarm water for a few minutes to help them more quickly reach room temperature.

2 • Warm the milk in the microwave for 30 seconds.

3 • In a small bowl, melt 3 tablespoons of the butter in the microwave, then let it cool. You can refrigerate it for a couple of minutes to cool the butter faster.

4 • In a large blender, combine the milk, melted butter, flour, water, sugar, vanilla, and salt and blend for 30 seconds. If there is flour still unmixed on the sides, use a silicone spatula to scrape down the sides and blend again for a few seconds until the batter is smooth. It may look watery. Pour it into a measuring cup with a spout. Place the batter in the refrigerator, covered, for a minimum of 30 minutes.

(RECIPE CONTINUES)

5 • Heat an 8-inch nonstick sauté pan over medium-high heat. Add a pat of the remaining butter and melt it evenly over the surface of the pan. Pour a thin layer of batter, a scant ¼ cup, into the pan and quickly spread it around by turning it with your wrist or using a wooden crepe spreader—the layer should be very thin. Cook until the edges are browned and crispy, about 3 minutes. Using a large spatula (and often your fingers, too—just don't burn yourself!), flip the crepe and cook until lightly browned on the second side, about 2 minutes. Keep an eye on the bottom of crepe and, if it's browning too quickly, reduce the heat to medium. Remove the crepe from the pan and set it aside on a large plate.

6 • With a butter knife, scoop a dollop of Nutella and gently spread a thin layer of it over the entire crepe. Roll the crepe and eat it while it's hot. Repeat.

7 • Making crepes in batches and stacking them up as you go is possible, but the crepes might lose some of their texture. Cook and serve as you go, or make a batch and, when it's time to serve, heat up the pan and warm the crepes individually before spreading the Nutella or fillings of choice.

COOK'S NOTE: *Additional filling suggestions:*

Butter, brown sugar, and cinnamon

Whipped cream and strawberries with powdered sugar sprinkled on top

Chocolate syrup, sliced bananas, and whipped cream

Peanut butter and jam or marmalade

THE YIN AND YANG OF BANANA BREAD (GLUTEN-FREE AND REGULAR)

PREP TIME: 10 MINUTES PLUS 10 MINUTES TO COOL

COOK TIME: 50 MINUTES

MAKES ONE 9-BY-5-INCH LOAF

My parents were wonderful cooks, but bakers they were not—they never baked a thing. An oven isn't needed for most of the Chinese dishes they made, and the Chinese steam their breads, buns, and sponge cakes. Out of necessity, I started baking when I was in my early thirties. I had started feeling exhausted all the time—no matter how much sleep I got, it never seemed like enough. I offhandedly told an actress colleague of mine, and she asked me if I ate a lot of pasta. I laughed. "Pasta? Of course! I'm Chinese—we invented pasta!" She persuaded me to cut out pasta and wheat for a week to see if I noticed a difference. Frankly, I thought it was nuts—don't Olympic athletes carb up before a workout?! The funny thing was, it worked. It was hard as hell—this was when the gluten-free revolution was in its infancy, so there weren't many products that didn't have gluten in them. But because I felt so much better, I dove into gluten-free baking like a mad scientist, experimenting with rice flours, almond flours, and far beyond. Even though I never got tested to see if I actually was intolerant, I do watch how much wheat and gluten I consume. And whenever I feel that peculiar brain fog, that fatigue and the ache in my joints, I know it's time for me to take a break. This recipe is one of the first I mastered when baking gluten-free, and it's deliciously nutty (though you can choose to leave out the nuts if you're not a fan). If you want an on-the-go treat, bake it in muffin tins and simply scale back your baking time.

GLUTEN-FREE BREAD:

Cooking spray

3 ripe bananas, mashed (about 1 cup)

3 large eggs

¼ cup agave or liquid sweetener

2 tablespoons granulated sugar

¼ cup vegetable oil or 4 tablespoons melted butter

1 teaspoon vanilla extract

3 cups almond flour

1 teaspoon ground cinnamon

1 teaspoon baking soda

1 teaspoon baking powder

1 teaspoon xanthan gum

¼ teaspoon kosher salt

1 cup finely chopped pecans or walnuts (optional)

Butter, ice cream, or whipped cream, for serving (optional)

1 • Preheat the oven to 350°F and move the cooking rack to the center position in the oven. Line a 9-by-5-inch loaf pan with parchment paper. Spray the bottom and sides of the paper with cooking spray.

2 • In a large bowl, add the mashed bananas, eggs, agave, sugar, oil, and vanilla. Whisk together until combined.

3 • In a separate large bowl, whisk the almond flour, cinnamon, baking soda, baking powder, xantham gum, and salt together until combined. Add the almond flour mixture to the batter incrementally, mixing gently with a spatula until combined. If using nuts, fold them into the batter.

4 • Pour the batter into the prepared loaf pan, place it into the oven, and bake for 50 minutes, or until a toothpick inserted in the center comes out clean. Cool it in the pan on a rack for 10 minutes, then pull the parchment paper away from the pan to gently remove the bread.

5 • When ready to serve, slice the bread with a serrated knife. Serve as is or with butter, ice cream, or whipped cream, if desired. The bread will keep at room temperature for up to 3 days. If freezing, slice it, insert parchment paper between each slice, wrap it with aluminum foil, and freeze. The loaf will stay good for several months frozen. Thaw it at room temperature for a few hours or defrost it in the microwave.

Banana Bread Muffins with Red Beans

PREP TIME: 15 MINUTES

COOK TIME: 25 MINUTES

MAKES 16 MUFFINS

1½ sticks unsalted butter, at room temperature

1 cup granulated sugar

½ cup packed dark brown sugar

3 large eggs

3 ripe bananas, mashed (about 1 cup)

3 cups all-purpose flour

1 teaspoon baking soda

1 teaspoon baking powder

1 teaspoon kosher salt

⅓ cup sour milk (⅓ cup milk and 1 teaspoon white vinegar) or buttermilk

1 cup finely chopped pecans

½ cup Sweet Red Beans (see page 81)

Fact is, despite my heroic efforts, not everyone likes gluten-free flour. Even when I was on my almost-total GF kick, I'd occasionally get lazy (again, you couldn't just buy it back then; I always had to make it!), and that's when you'd find me sitting down in acting class and eating an entire Sara Lee pound cake. My classmates still tease me about that to this day. I don't have celiac disease, so this was doable—and when I was younger, with my fast metabolism, I'd still stay skinny. But boy, do I make a mess when I bake. I don't know how the cooking shows do it. Every time I undertake a project, my whole kitchen is a catastrophe: measuring cups and flour everywhere, a sink filled with dirty bowls and utensils. These are worth the mess, though.

COOK'S NOTE: You can freeze these and then throw them into a toaster oven for a quick snack.

1 • Preheat the oven to 350°F. Line a cupcake pan with paper cupcake liners.

2 • In a large bowl and using an electric mixer, cream the butter with the granulated sugar and brown sugar until it's fluffy and light. Mix one egg at a time into the butter mixture. Add the mashed bananas and mix until incorporated.

3 • In a separate large bowl, whisk together the flour, baking soda, baking powder, and salt. Using a spatula, mix the flour mixture into the banana mixture, alternating with the sour milk. (Be sure to add the flour first and end with the flour.) Fold in the pecans and red beans.

4 • Scoop the batter into each prepared cupcake tin to fill almost to the top of the paper.

5 • Bake for 25 minutes or until a toothpick comes out clean. Place the cupcake pan on a rack to cool. When the muffins are cool enough to handle, remove them from the paper liners and allow them to cool completely on the rack.

CANDIED PECANS

PREP TIME: 5 MINUTES

COOK TIME: 10 MINUTES

MAKES ABOUT 2 CUPS

On Marvel's *Agents of S.H.I.E.L.D.*, many times we would shoot on location, and oftentimes, where we had to film was far from craft service. As Agent May, I often had fight scenes, so I burned a lot of calories and always felt peckish. The running joke on set was that if you needed to find Ming-Na, go to craft service. On the days when I couldn't get to the food, I needed to have food near me. The food also had to be healthy and able to get through a 12- to 15-hour workday without spoiling. Well, most of those non-spoilable foods are not the healthiest, like chips or cookies. And an apple or banana can satisfy only to a point when one has the munchies.

Now, I've always liked candied pecans, but they're usually too over-the-top sweet with too many other flavors jumbled in, such as nutmeg, which I don't particularly like. Always ready to experiment in the kitchen, I set out to make my own streamlined version. This recipe is simple, but I love the crunch and slight added sweetness. It's a healthy snack alone or mixed with other trail mixes. My mother loves them so much that whenever she visits, I always make an extra batch for her to take home. I like to think of her watching her favorite Chinese soap operas, munching on them and thinking about her favorite child. LOL (just kidding, bros!).

¼ cup granulated sugar

¼ cup packed light brown sugar

2 tablespoons water

½ teaspoon ground cinnamon

½ teaspoon pure vanilla extract

½ cup (2 ounces) palm sugar

8 ounces pecan halves

1 • In a large bowl, mix together the granulated sugar, light brown sugar, water, cinnamon, and vanilla. Set aside.

2 • In a medium bowl, melt the palm sugar in the microwave until softened to a thick honey consistency, starting with 1 minute, then intervals of 30 seconds. You can also melt it in a small saucepan on the stovetop with 1 tablespoon of water over medium-low heat, but be very careful not to burn it, stirring constantly.

3 • Add the pecan halves to the melted sugar, then add the sugar mixture and mix well.

4 • Place parchment paper in an air fryer and spread the pecans out in a single layer. Air-fry at 350°F for 7 minutes, until the coating is crunchy.

5 • Allow the pecans to cool on the parchment paper. If they're not crunchy enough, return them to the air fryer for an additional 2 minutes.

COOK'S NOTE: *If you do not have an air fryer, you can make them in the oven at 350°F, checking and turning every 10 minutes, until crunchy, for a total of about 30 minutes overall.*

PREP TIME: 25 MINUTES

COOK TIME: 30 MINUTES

SERVES: 8

MING'S VEGAN VEGETABLE SOUP

For me, this soup is all about the collard greens. I rarely see them in veggie soups, and I like the crunch they add. During my vegan days (yes, I go on a lot of diets—I know I'm not alone in this!), I ordered a soup like this at a vegan restaurant. Well, it was so incredible that I had to ask the chef what was in it. I then went home and tried making it for myself . . . with some Ming additions, of course. I added mung beans and napa cabbage to make it even heartier, as I was always a bit hungry when I was on a vegan kick—this kept me full and happy.

2 tablespoons extra-virgin olive oil

1 cup chopped yellow onion

3 garlic cloves, minced

3 carrots, peeled and cut into 1-inch pieces (about 2 cups)

3 stalks celery, sliced

1½ cups chopped napa cabbage, leafy top part separated from firm white bottom, divided

2 teaspoons kosher salt

1 teaspoon onion powder

1 teaspoon garlic powder

1 teaspoon mushroom bouillon powder

1 teaspoon ground cumin

½ teaspoon ground white pepper

1 bay leaf

3 cups vegetable broth plus 3 cups water

2 large bunches collard greens, ribs and stems removed, finely chopped (about 3 cups)

Juice of ½ lemon

1 (15-ounce) can black-eyed peas, drained and rinsed

1 cup mung beans, cooked (see Cook's Note)

½ cup canned sweet corn, drained and rinsed

1 cup soy milk

1 • In a large stockpot over medium-high heat, add the olive oil. Add the onion and cook, stirring constantly, to release the flavor, about 2 minutes. Then add the garlic and cook, stirring constantly, for 1 minute. Add the carrots, celery, and the white bottom part of the napa cabbage. Cook, stirring constantly, to sweat them, about 3 minutes. Add the salt, onion powder, garlic powder, mushroom bouillon powder, cumin, white pepper, and bay leaf. Add the vegetable broth and water and bring to a boil, then lower the heat to a simmer, for 5 minutes.

2 • Add the collard greens and lemon juice and let simmer for 5 minutes. Now, add the top part of the napa cabbage, the black-eyed peas, mung beans, and corn. Let simmer for 5 minutes. Add ½ cup of water if the soup level appears too low and simmer for another 5 minutes.

3 • Taste and add more salt if needed and try some of the collard greens to make sure they're tender and cooked but still have crunch. Add the soy milk and stir well to incorporate.

COOK'S NOTE: *Cooked mung beans can be bought canned (drain and rinse), frozen, or vacuum-packed in pouches in Asian markets. You can substitute canned black beans or kidney beans, depending on your preference.*

PREP TIME: 20 MINUTES PLUS 4 HOURS MARINATING

COOK TIME: 45 MINUTES

SERVES: 4 AS AN APPETIZER

HUBBY'S CHINESE CHICKEN WINGS

- 1 cup light soy sauce
- ⅓ cup honey
- 1 teaspoon toasted sesame oil
- 1 teaspoon Shaoxing Chinese cooking wine
- ½ teaspoon freshly ground black pepper
- ¼ teaspoon garlic salt
- 3 garlic cloves, minced
- 1 scallion, white and green parts, sliced
- 2 pounds chicken wings (about 12 wings)

My hubby always brags that he won my heart with these chicken wings. On one of our first dates, he brought me to a dark, secluded beach in Malibu for a picnic and I thought, *This is either really romantic or I am about to be murdered.* Thankfully, I'm still alive to tell you how romantic a gesture it was and that these wings can make you fall in love! They're a perfect balance of sweet and savory, with a small kick of black pepper. Double the recipe for a larger crowd or a tailgate. And if you're single, don't let that stop you—you can marinate the wings, cook them, and then freeze a few to batch them out. Just wrap them well in foil and defrost them overnight in the refrigerator when you've got the craving.

1 • In a medium bowl, add the soy sauce and pour in the honey, stirring until the honey dissolves into the sauce. Stir in the sesame oil, cooking wine, pepper, and garlic salt. Mix in the garlic and scallion.

2 • Transfer the chicken wings to a gallon-size resealable plastic bag. Pour in the marinade, seal the bag, and turn it over a few times to coat the wings well. Marinate in the fridge for a minimum of 4 hours.

3 • Preheat the oven to 400°F. Cover a baking sheet with aluminum foil.

4 • Spread the chicken wings out on the prepared baking sheet. Bake for 30 to 35 minutes, turning once after 15 minutes, until cooked through and caramelized.

5 • Transfer the wings to a serving plate and serve with extra napkins.

VEGGIE SANDWICH

PREP TIME: 10 MINUTES
COOK TIME: 5 TO 10 MINUTES
SERVES: 2

You're probably thinking, *What? Another vegetarian recipe?!* Well, let me tell you that this veggie sandwich will surprise you with how tasty it is. *Yes, it really is.* This sandwich has bright flavors, and on its own it's actually a hefty meal, but if you're really worried it won't be enough, you can always toss an egg onto it for extra protein.

2 teaspoons Simple Basil Pesto (see page 195)

4 slices sandwich bread (your choice)

2 slices mozzarella or other cheese of your choice

1 tablespoon Hummus (recipe follows)

2 teaspoons honey mustard

2 tablespoons unsalted butter or extra-virgin olive oil, divided

1 medium ripe tomato, sliced

½ avocado, thinly sliced

½ cup loosely packed fresh spinach leaves

1 English or regular cucumber, sliced thinly lengthwise

Kosher salt and freshly ground black pepper

Potato chips of your choice

1 • Spread the pesto on 2 slices of the bread, then place a slice of cheese on top of each. On the remaining 2 bread slices, spread the hummus and honey mustard.

2 • In a large skillet over medium-low heat, melt 1 tablespoon of the butter or heat 1 tablespoon of the olive oil. Place the bread slices with pesto and cheese in the pan, cheese side up. Cook until the bread is toasted to a golden brown and the cheese has melted, 3 to 4 minutes.

3 • Layer the tomato slices, avocado, and spinach on top of the cheese. Top the sandwiches with the hummus-and-mustard-spread slices of bread. Add the remaining butter or olive oil to the pan, then carefully flip the sandwiches to brown the other side. Remove the sandwiches from the pan when golden brown, another 3 minutes.

4 • Open the sandwiches to add the sliced cucumbers to each one and season them with a sprinkle of salt and pepper to taste. Close the sandwiches again and, if you like, use toothpicks to keep the filling together before cutting the sandwiches in half for serving.

5 • Serve immediately with chips.

Hummus

PREP TIME: 15 MINUTES

COOK TIME: 25 MINUTES

SERVES: 4 TO 6

MAKES ABOUT 1½ CUPS

1 (15-ounce) can chickpeas, drained and rinsed

½ teaspoon baking soda

2 garlic cloves, roughly chopped

½ cup fresh lemon juice

½ teaspoon kosher salt

2 tablespoons tahini

¼ teaspoon ground cumin

2 tablespoons extra-virgin olive oil, divided

¼ can black beans, drained, rinsed, and roughly chopped (optional)

3 to 4 pieces sun-dried tomatoes packed in oil, drained and chopped (optional)

1 teaspoon minced fresh parsley, for garnish

1 pinch paprika, for garnish

Pita chips, cut vegetables, or pita bread for serving

I was introduced to Middle Eastern food late in life. Having grown up mainly eating Chinese food and occasional American-style holiday food, we never ventured out into these culinary regions. Homemade hummus has become a staple in my kitchen, and it's so easy to make, there's no reason to buy it. It's great as a dip or spread but also with boiled eggs, in a salad, on a sandwich, and more—get creative!

1 • In a medium saucepan, add the chickpeas and enough water to cover. Add the baking soda and bring it to a boil over high heat. Lower the heat to a simmer and cook until the chickpeas shed their skins and are softened, 20 to 25 minutes.

2 • Meanwhile, in a food processor or blender, blend the garlic, lemon juice, and salt for 15 seconds or until smooth. Allow 5 to 10 minutes for the acid of the lemon to marinate the garlic, then add the tahini and cumin. Add 1 tablespoon of the olive oil, then 2 to 4 tablespoons of cold water, 1 tablespoon at a time, to the mixture and blend until very smooth and creamy.

3 • Drain and rinse the chickpeas well. Add the chickpeas to the mixture and blend until all the ingredients are completely incorporated. If the texture seems a bit dry, add more cold water, 1 tablespoon at a time. The consistency should be smooth but still thick, not runny or watery.

4 • The black beans or sun-dried tomatoes can either be blended together with the hummus at this time or just mixed into it by hand, if desired. Add more salt to taste.

5 • Depending on what you wish to serve with the hummus, spoon it into a medium-size bowl or onto a platter. Drizzle the remaining olive oil on top and sprinkle the hummus with parsley and paprika. Serve it with pita chips, veggies, or pita bread. Store it, covered, in the refrigerator, for up to 1 week.

FISH TACOS

PREP TIME: 30 MINUTES

COOK TIME: 10 MINUTES

SERVES: 6

FOR THE FISH:

½ teaspoon paprika

½ teaspoon cayenne pepper (optional)

½ teaspoon kosher salt

¼ teaspoon freshly ground black pepper

Pinch of ground cumin

5 (6-ounce) tilapia or salmon fillets

2 tablespoons extra-virgin olive oil

1 tablespoon unsalted butter

FOR THE TOPPING:

2 cups shredded red cabbage

1 bunch fresh cilantro leaves, chopped

3 medium ripe tomatoes, diced

½ cucumber, diced

½ medium red onion, diced

½ cup canned corn, drained

¼ cup canned diced pineapples, drained

½ teaspoon kosher salt

¼ teaspoon freshly ground black pepper

Pinch cayenne pepper (optional)

½ avocado, thinly sliced

Look, these may not be the most authentic tacos you'll find out there, but they are my tribute to one of the most beloved dishes in Los Angeles: the fish taco. These are super fun at a party, where you can set up a taco bar and let guests serve themselves. Kids also love to make their own tacos, and you can sneak some healthy stuff like cabbage onto their plates, which is always a win in my book.

1 • MAKE THE FISH: In a small bowl, mix together the paprika, cayenne (to taste, if desired), salt, pepper, and cumin. Pat the fish fillets dry with paper towels. Season all sides of the fish with the spice mixture.

2 • Heat the olive oil and butter in a large sauté pan over medium heat. Add the fillets and cook until just cooked through and flaky, 3 to 4 minutes on each side. Set aside.

3 • MAKE THE TOPPING: In a medium bowl, mix together the cabbage, cilantro, tomatoes, cucumber, onion, corn, and pineapple. Stir in the salt, pepper, and cayenne, if desired. Mix in the avocado. Set aside.

4 • MAKE THE SAUCE: In a medium bowl, mix together the sour cream, mayonnaise, lime juice, hot sauce, and garlic powder. Set aside.

(RECIPE & INGREDIENTS CONTINUE)

FOR THE SAUCE:

1 cup sour cream

½ cup mayonnaise

3 tablespoons fresh lime juice

½ tablespoon hot sauce (such as Tabasco)

2 teaspoons garlic powder

TO CONTINUE:

16 to 20 (6-inch) corn tortillas

Shredded or grated cheese (your choice, optional)

2 limes, sliced into wedges

5 • TO CONTINUE: In a large sauté pan over medium heat, warm the tortillas for about 1 minute per side. Working in batches, make the tacos (or let your guests make their own!). Tear or slice the fish fillets and place on the bottom of the warmed tortillas. Add some of the vegetable topping and sauce to each. Add the cheese of your choice, if desired, and squeeze some lime juice on top. Serve them on a large platter.

6 • Make more tacos as needed. You can save the rest for another day, but I doubt there will be leftovers!

PREP TIME: 30 MINUTES

COOK TIME: 45 MINUTES

SERVES: 5

SLOBBY JOES
WITH ONION RINGS

FOR SLOBBY JOES:

¼ cup vegetable oil

1 small yellow onion, diced

½ red bell pepper, cored and diced

½ green bell pepper, cored and diced

4 garlic cloves, minced

1 pound ground turkey

½ pound ground pork

¼ cup dry red wine

1 (15-ounce) can tomato sauce

5 tablespoons tomato paste (half a 6-ounce can)

¼ cup red wine vinegar

2 tablespoons dark brown sugar

2 tablespoons Worcestershire sauce

1 tablespoon paprika

1 teaspoon sriracha

1 teaspoon ground cumin

1 teaspoon kosher salt

½ teaspoon freshly ground black pepper

20 sweet Hawaiian rolls

I have always loved sloppy joes, though in our household we call them "slobby" because we're slobs when we eat them—ha! I came up with this miniature version when the kids were young and I wanted to find something easy to make and freeze in appropriate portion sizes. The meat mixture freezes beautifully, and the small Hawaiian rolls are the perfect size for kids. We also love to entertain, so this recipe does double duty as party food at our barbecues. You don't *have* to serve them topped with onion rings, but they do make the difference between ordinary sloppy joes and extra-gourmet slobby joes.

1 • MAKE THE SLOBBY JOES: To a large sauté pan over medium-high heat, add the vegetable oil. Add the onion and cook, stirring constantly, until translucent, about 7 minutes. Add the red and green bell pepper and garlic and cook, stirring, for another 1 minute. Then add the turkey and pork and cook, breaking up the meat with a spoon, until browned, about 8 minutes. Stir in the red wine to deglaze the pan.

2 • Stir in the tomato sauce, tomato paste, vinegar, brown sugar, Worcestershire sauce, paprika, sriracha, cumin, salt, and pepper. Reduce the heat to low and simmer until the sauce is reduced to your "slobby" liking and the flavors have melded, 20 to 30 minutes. Add a few tablespoons of water if the sauce becomes too dry or thick.

3 • MEANWHILE, MAKE THE ONION RINGS: Preheat the oven to 200°F.

4 • Cut the sweet onion into rounds of ¼-inch-thick slices.

5 • In a shallow bowl, whisk the egg and milk together. In a second shallow bowl, mix together the flour, garlic powder, salt, five-spice powder, and pepper.

(RECIPE & INGREDIENTS CONTINUE)

6 • In a medium pot or deep fryer, heat the oil over medium-high heat to 350°F. Dip the sliced onion rings in the milk mixture, then cover them with flour mixture. Carefully add the onion rings in batches to the hot oil and fry until golden brown, about 8 minutes. Set them aside on a paper towel–lined sheet pan and keep in the warm oven until ready to serve.

7 • Cut the rolls in half and toast them. Fill the rolls with the meat sauce and top with onion rings. Serve immediately.

COOK'S NOTE: *Like your rings super crispy? You can double-fry them or add a few tablespoons of panko breadcrumbs to the flour mixture.*

FOR THE ONION RINGS:

1 medium sweet onion

1 large egg

½ cup whole milk

2 cups all-purpose flour

1 teaspoon garlic powder

½ teaspoon kosher salt

¼ teaspoon five-spice powder

⅛ teaspoon freshly ground black pepper

2 cups vegetable, corn, or peanut oil

PREP TIME: 10 MINUTES

COOK TIME: 6 TO 10 MINUTES

SERVES: 4

PESTO SALMON

4 (8-ounce) salmon fillets

½ teaspoon kosher salt

¼ teaspoon freshly ground black pepper

2 tablespoons extra-virgin olive oil

¼ cup Simple Basil Pesto (recipe follows)

½ fresh lemon (optional)

Fresh cilantro or parsley, for garnish

I will never understand how restaurants manage to overcook salmon. After all, it comes with its own visual aid to tell you when it's done—it changes color! When cooking, look for the salmon to turn from a translucent deep orange or pink to an opaque lighter orange or pink. If your salmon is white, you've gone too far and it will be dry.

There's so much to like about this dish—it's healthy and it's super fast, plus you can easily buy pesto sauce if you don't have the time or energy to make your own. When I don't make my own pesto, I like to use Costco's Kirkland-brand basil pesto.

1 • Rinse the salmon fillets and pat dry with paper towels. Season all sides with the salt and pepper.

2 • Add the olive oil to a large sauté pan over medium heat and sear the fillets until just cooked through, 3 to 4 minutes on each side, taking care not to overcook. (Flip when the color change from dark to light pink reaches halfway up the fillet.) Note that once the fillet is removed from the heat, the salmon will continue to cook.

3 • Top the hot salmon with a layer of pesto. You can add a squeeze of lemon, if desired, and garnish with cilantro or parsley.

COOK'S NOTE: *You can tell if the salmon is done from a touch test as well. Press the fillet with your finger, and if it is not too soft and bounces back, then it is done. If it's already very firm and has no bounce at all, then it's overcooked.*

Simple Basil Pesto

PREP TIME: 10 MINUTES

COOK TIME: 5 MINUTES

MAKES 1½ CUPS

½ cup pine nuts or chopped walnuts

2 cups packed fresh basil leaves

5 garlic cloves, chopped

¾ cup extra-virgin olive oil

½ cup grated Parmesan cheese

1 tablespoon fresh lemon juice

¼ teaspoon kosher salt

¼ teaspoon freshly ground black pepper

Pesto was another recipe where I felt compelled to venture out of my comfort zone. I'd never really liked it because, let's face it, most store-bought pesto here is not fresh tasting. On my first trip to Italy, somebody insisted that I try the real thing, and I loved my first taste of proper pesto. The only solution was to make my own at home, and since it's an essentially no-cook, blended sauce, it was easy to learn. The key is the fresh basil, but you also need to use really good olive oil and Parmesan cheese.

1 • In a medium sauté pan over medium-low heat, lightly toast the pine nuts, stirring occasionally, for 3 to 4 minutes. Nuts burn easily, so watch closely and don't walk away.

2 • In a food processor, add the toasted nuts, basil, and garlic and pulse until combined. Continue processing, slowly adding the olive oil a little at a time. Turn the processor off to scrape down the sides with a rubber spatula as you go and continue processing until you reach your desired consistency. Add the Parmesan cheese, lemon juice, salt, and pepper and pulse until everything is fully incorporated.

3 • Transfer the pesto sauce to a glass jar and refrigerate; it keeps for up to 1 week. If you're not going to use it within a few days, just freeze it in ice cube trays for later use. When you defrost it, please do not put it in the microwave, as it will make a mess with the oil and nuts. Just fill a large bowl with a few inches of hot water. Put the pesto cubes in a smaller bowl and place that bowl in the larger bowl. Allow the gentle heat to melt the cubes, stirring occasionally.

SHRIMP
WITH GARLIC NOODLES

PREP TIME: 5 MINUTES

COOK TIME: 10 MINUTES

SERVES: 4

This recipe was born out of yet another Ming-Na restaurant interrogation (I'm nice, I swear!) where I asked the chef for the recipe so I could make it at home, tweaked to my liking. I was intrigued by the restaurant's version because they used Chinese egg noodles, like you might have with lo mein, instead of Italian spaghetti or linguine. For me, the Chinese egg noodles give this a heartier and drier consistency. If you don't have egg noodles, don't sweat it, as other noodles in your pantry will work—this is a flexible recipe.

1 bag Chinese egg noodles (can also use 1 12-ounce box of regular linguine noodles)

3 tablespoons extra-virgin olive oil, divided

6 tablespoons butter (salted or unsalted), divided

7 to 8 garlic cloves, minced or pressed, divided

1 pound large (preferably 31/35 or 36/40) raw shrimp, shelled and deveined

½ fresh lemon, divided

1 tablespoon garlic powder

2 teaspoons kosher salt

¼ teaspoon ground white pepper

1 scallion, chopped, or 1 tablespoon chopped fresh parsley, for garnish (optional)

1 • Rinse the noodles under hot water. Drain the noodles in a colander and set aside. (If using regular linguine noodles, cook as directed to al dente, drain, and set aside.)

2 • In a sauté pan over medium heat, add 1 tablespoon of the olive oil and 1 tablespoon of the butter, swirling until it melts. Stir in about 1 teaspoon of the garlic, making sure it does not burn. Add the shrimp and cook, stirring constantly, until opaque, 2 to 3 minutes. Squeeze some lemon juice over the shrimp, then set aside to prevent overcooking.

3 • Add the remaining olive oil, butter, and garlic to the pan over medium heat. Cook the garlic, stirring constantly, until fragrant, about 1 minute. Add the noodles, then the garlic powder, salt, and white pepper. Return the shrimp to the pan and toss all the ingredients together.

4 • Garnish with chopped scallions or parsley, if desired. Squeeze more lemon juice over the dish and serve hot.

PREP TIME: 20 MINUTES

COOK TIME: 15 MINUTES

SERVES: 4

PASTA ARRABBIATA
ALLA HOLLYWOOD

1 tablespoon plus 1 teaspoon kosher salt, divided

1 (1-pound) package linguine or spaghetti

¼ cup extra-virgin olive oil

3 garlic cloves, minced

2 teaspoons red pepper flakes

1 (14.5-ounce) can diced tomatoes, drained, tomato water reserved

1 medium ripe tomato, chopped

2 tablespoons tomato paste

2 teaspoons sriracha

3 tablespoons chopped fresh basil leaves

1 cup freshly grated Parmesan cheese, divided

½ cup finely chopped fresh parsley, for garnish

It was 1993, and *The Joy Luck Club* had just premiered. I decided it was a good time to venture out to LA and check out the Hollywood vibe. I was a New Yorker, loved Manhattan, and never really considered living anywhere else. During this visit, I couldn't have expected that I would eventually make the big life decision to move to Hollywood and give my film and television career a chance. I always envisioned myself being a stage actress, working in theaters and on Broadway. When I came out and met with my LA agent, she took me to a fancy lunch where there was a spicy pasta dish on the menu. Back in the early nineties, this was a new concept! *How very LA!* I thought. Being the ever-adventurous foodie, I had to try it. This is one of my first LA food memories, my *Ratatouille* of Hollywood moment. So now, every time I have pasta arrabbiata, it takes me back to my first visit to LA. More than three decades later, it is certainly my home (though in my heart, I will always consider myself a New Yorker).

1 • Bring a large pot of water to a boil, add 1 tablespoon of the salt, then add the pasta and cook according to package instructions minus 1 minute. Reserve the pasta water for later use. Using tongs or pasta forks, transfer the pasta to an ice water bath to stop the cooking, drain, and set aside. Keep the pasta water hot.

2 • Heat the olive oil in a large skillet over medium heat. Add the garlic and red pepper flakes and cook, stirring constantly, until fragrant, about 1 minute. Add the diced tomatoes, fresh tomato, tomato paste, and sriracha, stirring constantly. Bring to a simmer, then lower the heat to medium-low and cook, stirring frequently, for 8 minutes. If needed, add the reserved tomato water 1 tablespoon at a time to loosen the sauce. Turn off the heat and stir in the basil and the remaining 1 teaspoon of salt.

3 • When ready to serve, return the reserved pasta water to a boil and dunk the cold pasta for 30 seconds. Drain well and plate, topped with sauce, Parmesan, and parsley. Add more red pepper for greater spice!

JAPCHAE
WITH CHICKEN

PREP TIME: 15 MINUTES

COOK TIME: 18 MINUTES

SERVES: 4

FOR THE SEASONED CHICKEN:

½ tablespoon cornstarch

2 teaspoons light soy sauce

2 teaspoons vegetable oil

½ teaspoon dark mushroom soy sauce

1 pound boneless skinless chicken breast, thinly sliced

FOR THE NOODLE MARINADE:

¼ cup light soy sauce

1 tablespoon toasted sesame oil

2 teaspoons minced garlic cloves

½ teaspoon sriracha

½ teaspoon kosher salt

8 ounces Korean sweet potato noodles

FOR THE STIR-FRY:

3 tablespoons vegetable oil, divided

2 medium carrots, peeled and julienned

1 red bell pepper, cored and sliced

1 cup sliced white mushrooms

1 cup sliced napa cabbage

2 garlic cloves, minced

1 cup packed fresh spinach leaves

1 tablespoon oyster sauce

1 tablespoon light soy sauce

1 teaspoon rice vinegar

⅛ teaspoon ground white pepper

I never knew noodles could be made out of sweet potato starch until about fifteen years ago when I was looking for gluten-free noodles and discovered dangmyeon in a Korean market. They're the base for all japchae and have a nice bite to them. Unlike other gluten-free or rice-based noodles that easily break apart, these keep their shape the next day, and you can successfully reheat leftovers. Experiment as I have and try using different meats and vegetables—the options are endless, and they'll become a go-to for you as well.

1 • **MAKE THE CHICKEN SEASONING:** In a large bowl, combine the cornstarch, light soy sauce, vegetable oil, and mushroom soy sauce. Add the chicken and toss to coat. Set it aside in the refrigerator.

2 • **MAKE THE NOODLE MARINADE:** Whisk together the light soy sauce, sesame oil, garlic, sriracha, and salt. Set aside.

3 • Bring a large pot of water to a boil. Add the noodles and cook for 6 minutes or 1 minute under package instructions. The noodles should be soft but chewy (al dente), just slightly undercooked. Drain the noodles, then return them to the pot. Pour in the noodle marinade and set aside.

4 • **BEGIN THE STIR-FRY:** Add 2 tablespoons of the vegetable oil to a large wok over medium-high heat, then add the seasoned chicken breast slices in a single layer. Let them sit until lightly seared, 1 to 2 minutes, before turning and cooking for 1 to 2 minutes on the other side. Then cook, stirring constantly, until cooked through, an additional 2 minutes. Remove the chicken from the wok and set aside on a plate.

5 • Add the remaining 1 tablespoon of oil to the wok, add the carrots, and cook, stirring constantly, for 2 minutes. Add the bell pepper, mushrooms, napa cabbage, and garlic and cook, stirring constantly, until the vegetables are cooked but crisp, about 2 minutes. Then add the spinach and cook, stirring, until it wilts, 30 to 60 seconds. Add the chicken and noodles, along with the oyster sauce, soy sauce, rice vinegar, and white pepper and stir-fry to mix well.

6 • Remove from the heat, transfer to a plate, and serve.

PREP TIME: 10 MINUTES

COOK TIME: 1 HOUR

SERVES: 1 OR 2

CORNISH HEN
WITH PLUM AND ORANGE SAUCE

- 1 (1½-pound) Cornish game hen
- 1 tablespoon extra-virgin olive oil
- 1 teaspoon kosher salt
- ¼ teaspoon freshly ground black pepper
- ¼ cup Chinese plum sauce
- 3 tablespoons fresh-squeezed orange juice
- 1 tablespoon light soy sauce
- 1 garlic clove, minced
- 1 teaspoon cornstarch
- ½ teaspoon agave syrup
- ¼ teaspoon Dijon mustard
- ¼ teaspoon fresh lemon juice
- 4 drops dark mushroom soy sauce
- 2 orange slices
- Fresh cilantro, for garnish (optional)

When I moved to New York, I was always on the hunt for easy recipes to make in my cramped apartment. One day I purchased some Cornish hens on a whim but didn't really know what to do with them. (I think I first learned about them on TV and they impressed me—I'd never had them growing up.) There I was, trying to be an adult all by myself; I felt *so* sophisticated. This is what I came up with, and they were a huge hit at my dinner parties. So, if you're looking for something exciting to serve at your next gathering, try this. Extra guests? Put more hens on the baking sheet and add an additional 5 minutes cooking time per hen!

1 • Preheat the oven to 375°F. Cover a baking sheet with foil for easy cleanup.

2 • Remove the giblets if there are some inside the hen. Rinse well and pat dry. Place the hen on the prepared baking sheet. Rub the hen all over with the olive oil. Season with the salt and pepper, inside and out.

3 • In a medium bowl, mix together the plum sauce, orange juice, light soy sauce, garlic, cornstarch, agave, mustard, lemon juice, and dark mushroom soy sauce. Let it sit for a few minutes.

4 • Coat the outside and the inside cavity of the hen with the sauce, reserving some for basting.

5 • Place the hen breast side down and cover it with sheet of aluminum foil. Roast for 30 minutes. Remove the foil cover. Brush more sauce over the hen. Flip it over and coat the breast side with sauce. Roast it for another 15 minutes.

6 • Brush any remaining sauce over the entire hen again. Carefully lift up the hen using long-handled tongs and slide the slices of orange underneath, breast side still up. Roast 15 more minutes. Check for doneness; the internal temperature should be 165°F or above. Transfer the hen to a serving dish and garnish with cilantro, if desired.

TURKEY OR VEGETABLE PATTIES
WITH PESTO AND SRIRACHA MAYO

PREP TIME: 30 MINUTES

COOK TIME: 20 MINUTES

MAKES 16 PATTIES

This recipe was inspired by a visit to a really nice vegan restaurant when I was on my vegan kick. I surgically dissected my patty and realized the restaurant used yam to hold the patties together, so, as I often do (following in my parents' footsteps), I went home and experimented. Even though I liked the veggie patties I made—I think they were better than the restaurant's!—my kids wanted meat, so I started making them with turkey. Don't get intimidated by the long list of ingredients. Once everything is chopped up and your veggies are cooked, you're just making a humble patty (and you can use a food processor to cut down time when mincing the veggies).

FOR THE VEGETABLE MEDLEY:

1 cup (4 ounces) broccoli florets

4 Brussels sprouts, trimmed and quartered

2 tablespoons extra-virgin olive oil

½ medium yellow onion, minced

3 garlic cloves, minced

½ cup frozen cauliflower, defrosted and drained, minced

½ cup canned sweet corn, drained

½ teaspoon kosher salt

⅛ teaspoon ground white pepper

1 • Cut about a dozen 5-by-5-inch parchment paper squares. Set aside.

2 • MAKE THE VEGETABLE MEDLEY: Place the broccoli and Brussels sprouts in a food processor or blender and blend until finely minced. Remove and set aside.

3 • In a large skillet or wok, heat the olive oil over medium-high heat. Add the onion and cook, stirring constantly, until tender, about 3 minutes. Add the garlic and cook, stirring constantly, until fragrant, 1 minute. Add the broccoli-and-Brussels-sprouts blend, the minced cauliflower, and corn and cook, stirring constantly, until tender, about 5 minutes. Stir in the salt and pepper. Transfer the vegetables to a large bowl and set aside to cool.

4 • MAKE THE TURKEY PATTIES: In a medium bowl, season the ground turkey with light soy sauce, mushroom soy sauce, salt, and white pepper. Set aside.

5 • Add the mashed yams and kabocha to the cooked vegetable medley and mix well. Add the seasoned ground turkey to the vegetable medley and mix well. (See Cook's Notes if you wish to just make veggie patties.) Form 16 palm-size patties, about 3 inches wide and 1 inch thick.

(RECIPE & INGREDIENTS CONTINUE)

6 • Place a piece of parchment paper between each patty. You can make stacks of them this way and wrap them with plastic wrap or aluminum foil to keep until ready to cook. You can also freeze the patties this way for later use.

7 • When ready to cook the patties, in a shallow bowl, beat the eggs with 2 teaspoons of water. Put the panko on one plate and the plain breadcrumbs on another. Dip the patties into the plain bread crumbs first, then dip them into the egg, then coat the patties thoroughly with panko.

8 • Heat a large skillet with 1 tablespoon of the oil over medium-high heat. Add batches of 3 patties at a time to the skillet. Cook until lightly golden on one side, about 2 minutes, then flip and cook for another 2 minutes. Lower the heat to medium and repeat the process, flipping the patties every 1 to 2 minutes until cooked through, for a total cook time of about 10 minutes. Add more oil if needed. This method helps to prevent the panko from burning, while allowing the interior of the patties to cook through. Repeat until all the patties are cooked.

9 • MAKE THE SRIRACHA MAYO: In a small bowl, mix together the mayonnaise, agave, sriracha, and lemon juice, if using.

10 • To serve, spread 1 tablespoon of sriracha mayo on a plate and smear it into a circle about 4 inches wide. Place a patty on top of the mayo, add a 1 teaspoon dollop of sriracha mayo on top of the patty, then add 1 teaspoon of pesto to the center of the mayo. Add a dot of sriracha hot sauce to garnish.

COOK'S NOTES: *For veggie-only patties, replace the turkey with 1 additional cup of yams and form the patties. Follow the same steps for cooking.*

If you do not have a food processor, simply mince the broccoli and Brussels sprouts for the medley.

FOR THE TURKEY PATTIES:

1 pound lean ground turkey

½ tablespoon light soy sauce

1 teaspoon dark mushroom soy sauce

½ teaspoon kosher salt

¼ teaspoon ground white pepper

1 cup steamed or boiled peeled, mashed yams

1 cup steamed or boiled peeled, mashed kabocha (Japanese pumpkin)

2 large eggs

2 cups panko breadcrumbs

2 cups plain breadcrumbs

3 tablespoons extra-virgin olive oil, divided

FOR THE SRIRACHA MAYO:

4 tablespoons Japanese or Kewpie mayonnaise, but regular works as well

1 tablespoon agave syrup

½ teaspoon sriracha, plus more for garnish

¼ teaspoon fresh lemon juice (optional)

Simple Basil Pesto (see page 195)

PREP TIME: 20 MINUTES

COOK TIME: 30 MINUTES

SERVES: 6

NO-FAIL CHICKEN PARMESAN

1 (16-ounce) box linguine

1 (24-ounce) jar marinara sauce

1 cup panko breadcrumbs

3 teaspoons garlic powder, divided

1 teaspoon kosher salt, divided

1 cup plain breadcrumbs

1½ cups finely grated Parmesan, divided

2 large eggs

1 teaspoon dried oregano

3 boneless skinless chicken breasts

½ teaspoon freshly ground black pepper

1 cup corn or vegetable oil

2 cups shredded mozzarella cheese

I didn't start cooking Italian food until I had my kids; I wanted to learn how to make the dishes they loved from their favorite restaurants. I think I preferred to cook Chinese food when I was single because so many of our dishes involve using only one wok or pot. With Italian, I always find myself using so many pots and pans! There's a pot to boil the noodles, a pan to sauté the garlic and onions, and another pot to simmer the sauce. I hated the chore of washing them all after cooking. Being a mom changed my perspective, because the reward of seeing my kids enjoy eating these dishes makes the extra cleanup completely worthwhile. I guess that's a mother's love, right? I've added panko to the breading, as I am always looking for extra crunch—it's so satisfying.

1 • Bring a large pot of water to a boil. Add the linguine and cook according to the instructions on the package minus 1 minute, so that the pasta is al dente. Using tongs or pasta forks, remove the pasta from the hot water, reserving the water for later use. Rinse the pasta in a strainer under cold water. You can also transfer the pasta to a bowl of ice water to completely stop it from continuing to cook. Drain again and set aside.

2 • Add the marinara to a medium saucepan over medium-high heat and bring to a boil, then turn off the heat.

3 • On a large plate, mix together the panko, 2 teaspoons of the garlic powder, and ¼ teaspoon of the salt. On another large plate, mix together the plain breadcrumbs, ½ cup of the Parmesan cheese, and the remaining teaspoon of garlic powder. In a large, shallow bowl, whisk the eggs and oregano with 2 tablespoons of water.

4 • Pat the chicken breasts dry. Butterfly-slice each breast, then slice each one down the middle to divide into 2 thin pieces or cutlets.

(RECIPE CONTINUES)

5 • Place a damp paper towel underneath the cutting board to prevent shifting and a sheet of plastic wrap on top of the board. Place the chicken on the plastic wrap and place another sheet of plastic wrap over the chicken. (Or put the chicken in gallon-size resealable bags or plastic produce bags and lay it flat.) Put as many pieces as will fit on the cutting board.

6 • Using the flat side of a meat mallet or a rolling pin, lightly pound the breasts to thin them a little more. The plastic wrap will keep the chicken meat from splattering juice everywhere. Always make sure to thoroughly wash your hands with soap and water after touching raw chicken.

7 • Lightly season both sides of the breasts with the remaining ¾ teaspoon of salt and the pepper.

8 • Have your dredging station ready next to your skillet in the order of panko, eggs, and plain breadcrumbs with Parmesan, with the panko closest to the pan. On the other side, have a baking sheet fitted with a rack to drain oil from the fried chicken breasts or line a large platter with some paper towels. Move the oven rack to the top level.

9 • Heat the vegetable oil in a large skillet over medium-high heat to 350° to 365°F.

10 • Using metal tongs, grab a chicken breast, dredge it in the eggs and drip off the excess. Then place the chicken in the plain breadcrumb mixture, making sure it is completely covered on both sides, and shake off the excess. Dip the chicken back into the eggs, covering both sides, then dip it into the panko. Grab a handful of the panko and completely coat the chicken.

11 • Gently place the coated chicken in the hot oil and cook both sides until golden brown, about 1 minute per side. I usually do 2 breasts at a time. Monitor the heat of the oil and lower the heat if the oil starts to smoke. Remove the breasts from the oil and let them drip off the excess, then transfer them to the wire rack or paper towels. Repeat for each chicken breast.

12 • Meanwhile, bring the pasta water back to a boil and preheat the broiler.

13 • Place the fried chicken on a sheet pan and top with the mozzarella cheese. Move the sheet pan to the broiler for 1 minute, keeping an eye on the cheese to prevent burning. Once the cheese has melted and browned, remove the sheet pan.

14 • Return the pasta to the boiling water for 30 seconds to reheat, then drain.

15 • To serve, plate the pasta and top with a generous amount of marinara sauce. Garnish with Parmesan cheese. Top with one chicken breast or put the breast next to the pasta, so it doesn't get soggy. Add more pasta sauce on top and finish with more Parmesan cheese. Serve immediately.

CHICKEN MARSALA

PREP TIME: 25 MINUTES

COOK TIME: 20 MINUTES

SERVES: 4

2 boneless skinless chicken breasts

2 teaspoons kosher salt, divided

1 teaspoon freshly ground black pepper, divided

1 teaspoon dried oregano

1 teaspoon dried basil

1 cup all-purpose flour

2 large eggs, beaten

5 tablespoons extra-virgin olive oil, divided

4 to 5 tablespoons unsalted butter, divided

½ sweet onion, chopped

12 ounces white button mushrooms, thinly sliced

2 teaspoons garlic powder

⅔ cup Marsala wine

1 (14-ounce) can chicken broth

⅔ cup whole milk or nondairy milk

1 (16-ounce) box of angel hair or linguine pasta

2 tablespoons chopped fresh Italian parsley, for garnish

Two things Eric and I are most proud of when it comes to raising our kids are instilling in them a love for food and for eighties music. Music aside, one fun part of eating out with the kids when they were younger was discovering new foods that they liked. One of those discoveries was chicken marsala. So, of course, I had to learn to make that at home for them. Now, when we go out to eat and they order marsala, they always say, "Mom, yours is so much better." (I didn't even have to bribe them to say that.) So often, restaurants serve dry, paper-thin chicken that they call marsala and charge too much. I make mine with a lot of sauce and a ton of mushrooms so that you get sauce+mushroom+chicken in every bite. Restaurant Daughter Rule #1: NEVER HOLD BACK, AND NEVER MAKE SKIMPY MEALS!

1 • Rinse the chicken breasts, then pat them dry with paper towels. Butterfly-slice each chicken breast, then slice each one down the middle to divide into two thin pieces or cutlets.

2 • Place a damp paper towel underneath the cutting board to prevent shifting and a sheet of plastic wrap on top of the board. Place the chicken on the plastic wrap and place another sheet of plastic wrap over the chicken. (Or put the chicken in gallon-size resealable bags or plastic produce bags and lay them flat.) Put as many pieces as will fit on the cutting board.

3 • Using the flat side of a meat mallet or a rolling pin, lightly pound the breasts to thin them a little more. The plastic wrap will keep the chicken meat from splattering juice everywhere.

4 • Sprinkle 1 teaspoon of the salt, ½ teaspoon of the pepper, and the oregano and basil on both sides of the breasts.

5 • Add the flour to a shallow bowl and the eggs to a second shallow bowl.

(RECIPE CONTINUES)

6 • Bring a large pot of water to a boil. Once boiling, lower the heat to simmer. Keep the water hot, ready for cooking the pasta later.

7 • Dip all the chicken cutlets into the eggs, thoroughly coating each piece. Set aside.

8 • Line a sheet pan with paper towels. In a large skillet over medium-high heat, heat 2 tablespoons of the olive oil and melt 2 tablespoons of the butter. Coat each chicken breast in flour, shaking off the excess, and place as many as you can comfortably fit in the skillet. Cook until golden brown, 2 to 3 minutes per side, taking care to not overcook—slightly undercooking is better as they will go back into the skillet later for further cooking. Transfer the chicken to the paper towel-lined sheet pan to absorb excess oil. Add a little more oil and butter to the pan and continue to coat and cook the remaining chicken.

9 • In the same skillet, heat ½ tablespoon of the olive oil, then add the onion and cook, stirring constantly, until lightly translucent, about 6 minutes. Lower the heat to medium, add the mushrooms, and cook, stirring constantly, until tender, 5 to 6 minutes.

10 • Add ½ tablespoon of the olive oil and ½ tablespoon of the butter, the remaining 1 teaspoon of salt and ½ teaspoon of pepper, and the garlic powder to the skillet and stir to combine. Raise the heat to medium-high, add the Marsala wine, and cook it down until it's reduced by half, stirring and scraping the bottom of the pan to incorporate the browned bits into the sauce.

11 • Add the broth and milk of choice. Lower the heat to a simmer, cover the pan, and cook until the sauce thickens slightly, a reduction by a fourth at most. (My kids and I LOVE the sauce, so make sure there's plenty available if you love sauce, too. Don't reduce too much or overly thicken the sauce.)

12 • Add the chicken back to the skillet, add the remaining butter, and simmer, covered, for 5 minutes. Spoon the sauce over the chicken. If the sauce is too watery, you can whisk in a little flour to thicken it. Turn off the heat and allow the chicken to sit in the sauce.

13 • Bring the pot of water back to a boil and salt the water. Cook the pasta according to the instructions on the package minus 1 minute so that it's al dente.

14 • Place the pasta on a plate with chicken marsala on top. Garnish with parsley.

COOK'S NOTE: *I like my food HOT. If you're not eating this right away, use tongs or pasta forks to remove the pasta from the hot water. Rinse the pasta in a strainer under cold water. You can also transfer the pasta for a minute or two into a bowl of ice water to completely stop it from continuing to cook. Then dunk the pasta in reheated pasta water for 30 seconds before serving.*

ROASTED CHICKEN CONGEE

PREP TIME: 30 MINUTES

COOK TIME: 30 MINUTES

SERVES: 6

- 1 whole roasted rotisserie chicken
- ½ cup uncooked long-grain or jasmine rice
- ¼ cup uncooked glutinous rice (sticky rice) or sweet rice
- 1 (14.5-ounce) can chicken broth
- 1 teaspoon kosher salt
- ¼ teaspoon ground white pepper

Congee, a creamy rice porridge, is a wonderful staple in Chinese comfort food. When my mom, brother, and I lived in New York City, we always went to Chinatown and ate at Big Wong. They had the most flavorful congee with the best stock and smooth consistency, and they always served it with youtiao, long, fried pieces of dough that were super crispy and salty. We'd dunk the youtiao in the congee for added texture, and it was so ridiculously good.

At home, my family and I like to eat rotisserie chicken, and we always have leftovers, which is perfect for adding to homemade congee. That said, I don't want to spend hours over a stove waiting for the congee to thicken, which is what you must do if you make it in the traditional way. I thought it over; rice is just starch, right? Why don't I just blend the mixture to thicken it? So I tried it out, and it turned out great! I even served my congee to my mom, who couldn't believe that my magic trick had worked so well. If you've ever been intimidated by the thought of making congee, try this out! You'll think, "Ming-Na is a genius!" LOL.

1 • Using cooking-prep disposable gloves if you don't like the feel of the meat and grease on your bare hands, remove as much chicken meat from the bones as possible. Separate the skin from the meat and set aside.

2 • Place all the bones and the carcass in a large pot and fill with enough water to cover the bones. Bring it to boil, then lower the heat to a simmer and cook for 30 minutes.

3 • Mix together the two different rices, rinse well, and drain.

4 • Chop all the dark meat and about 1½ cups of the white meat into small pieces. Set aside. Place the remaining chicken breast meat in a covered container and refrigerate for use in other recipes.

(RECIPE CONTINUES)

5 • Scrape the reserved skin with a knife to remove and discard as much fat as possible. Then finely chop the skin. Set aside.

6 • After simmering the bones, remove them from the pot. At this point, you're looking for about 3 cups of broth to remain in the pot. Add the mixed rice to the bone broth. Bring to a boil, then lower the heat to a simmer with enough heat to keep the broth slightly percolating. Cover but place chopsticks (or something similar) under the lid or leave the lid slightly askew to allow for ventilation while cooking. If it doesn't seem like there's enough broth, add another ½ cup of canned chicken broth. Keep an eye on the rice to make sure it does not get too dry but DO NOT STIR the rice for 15 minutes.

7 • Check to see if the rice is fully cooked; it should still be more wet than regular cooked rice. Use an immersion blender that has a flat head to grind the rice mixture to a smooth consistency. If you don't own an immersion blender, then carefully pour the hot rice broth into a blender and pulse to a smooth consistency, adding water or chicken broth if needed. If using a blender, add the rice back into the pot after blending.

8 • Add the skin to the pot over medium-high heat and cook for 5 minutes. Stir in the chicken meat. Add more water or chicken broth, as needed, until the consistency is like soft oatmeal or to your liking. Season with salt and pepper.

9 • Serve hot.

COOK'S NOTES: *If you use a supermarket rotisserie chicken, I recommend rinsing off some of the spices that are on the skin, because you don't necessarily want all the weird seasonings they use. I like the Costco one because it's not overly spiced.*

When this congee is refrigerated, it will get thicker. Just add a little water to it when you reheat.

PREP TIME: 10 MINUTES

COOK TIME: 10 MINUTES

SERVES: 4

FRENCH VIETNAMESE BLACK PEPPER STEAK

1 teaspoon light soy sauce

½ teaspoon dark mushroom soy sauce

1 teaspoon cornstarch

1½ tablespoons plus 1 teaspoon vegetable oil, divided

1 pound ribeye steak, cut into 1½-inch cubes and trimmed of fat

1 medium yellow onion, chopped into 1½-inch pieces

1 whole scallion, cut in half

2 (¼-inch) slices of peeled ginger (about the diameter of a quarter)

1 tablespoon black pepper sauce (I use Lee Kum Kee)

1 teaspoon Shaoxing Chinese cooking wine

½ teaspoon kosher salt

½ teaspoon freshly ground black pepper

Cooked white rice, for serving (see page 236)

You can never go wrong with steak and onions, in my humble opinion. I first had this dish, also known as shaking beef, at a Vietnamese restaurant, and after the first bite I thought, *OH! Why haven't I ever made this before?!* The black pepper sauce is the star of the show here—it makes for an aromatic dish that is flavorful and a little spicy but not *too-hot* spicy, and delivers big flavors.

1 • In a medium bowl, mix together the light soy sauce, dark mushroom soy sauce, cornstarch, and 1 teaspoon of the vegetable oil. Add the steak and toss it to season.

2 • Heat a wok over high heat and add ½ tablespoon of the oil. Add the onion and cook, stirring constantly, until lightly transparent, about 5 minutes. Set aside.

3 • Add 1 tablespoon of the oil to the wok, add the scallion and ginger to flavor the oil, then add the seasoned ribeye. Sear the meat for about 1 minute on one side. Flip the steak pieces and sear the other side for 1 minute. Then cook the steak, stirring constantly, until cooked to medium or to your liking, 2 to 3 more minutes.

4 • Splash the sides of the wok with 1 tablespoon of water. Stir in the black pepper sauce. Splash the sides of the wok with the cooking wine and add the reserved onion, salt, and pepper. Mix all the ingredients together and cook for another 1 minute.

5 • Transfer to a serving dish and serve with rice.

BIRD'S NEST

PREP TIME: 1 MINUTE

COOK TIME: 3 MINUTES

SERVES: 4

4 slices bread, your choice

3 tablespoons plus 1 teaspoon unsalted butter, divided

5 large eggs

¼ teaspoon kosher salt, divided

¼ teaspoon freshly ground black pepper, divided

¼ cup maple syrup, divided, for serving

I was a new mom, taking my daughter, Michaela, to her preschool, where I befriended a fellow New Yorker, Suzanna. I was visiting with her one morning after we'd dropped off our kids when she generously offered to make breakfast. "I'll make you a bird's nest," she said. I was confused at first because there's a Chinese dish called bird's nest that consists of deep-fried noodles (the nest) with seafood and vegetables piled in the center. Oh, and there's also a Chinese soup with the same name, but it's a complicated banquet dish. Neither of these dishes was meant for breakfast or is easy to whip up! But when she made her bird's nest, it clicked for me. The name came about because a hole is cut out of a slice of bread with a cookie cutter, then an egg is cracked into the hole, where it sits like a bird in its nest! So clever and cute! We have remained great friends to this day, and I dedicate this recipe to our enduring friendship as our little chicks are now leaving their nests.

While working on this book, I talked with others, and, it turns out, there are lots of different names for this dish: egg in the basket, toad in the hole, egg in a hole, hole in one, one-eyed Jack, framed eggs, egg in a trash can—the list goes on. What do you call it?

1 • Using a round cookie cutter a bit smaller than the width of your slices of bread, cut out round circles in the center of each of the slices. Reserve the cut-out circles for later.

2 • Melt 1 tablespoon of the butter in a medium skillet over medium-high heat. Place a slice of bread, which now has a hole in the center, in the skillet. Melt ½ teaspoon of the butter in the bread's hole. Crack open an egg and carefully drop it into the hole of the bread. Check to see if the bread is toasting and turn down the heat if you fear it may burn. Depending on how you like your eggs, cook for 2 to 3 minutes.

(RECIPE CONTINUES)

3 • Place another ½ teaspoon of the butter on top of the yolk, then flip the bread and egg over to cook the other side, an additional 1 to 2 minutes. Season with salt and pepper. Remove from heat and repeat with the remaining 3 slices of bread and 3 more eggs.

4 • In a small bowl, beat the remaining egg with 1 tablespoon of water. In a medium sauté pan, melt 1 tablespoon of the butter over medium-high heat. Coat the 4 bread circles in the beaten egg. Place them in the pan and cook until lightly browned, turning once, a total of 4 to 6 minutes. You've made mini–French toast rounds!

5 • To serve, place the rounds of French toast over the bird's nests and serve with very small (prep-size) bowls of maple syrup on the plate, for dipping.

PREP TIME: 15 MINUTES

COOK TIME: 1 HOUR

SERVES: 5; MAKES 8 ROLLS

LASAGNA ROLL-UPS

10 long lasagna noodles

4 tablespoons extra-virgin olive oil, divided

10 ounces lean ground beef or turkey

3 tablespoons diced onion

2 garlic cloves, minced

1 teaspoon kosher salt, divided

¼ teaspoon ground white pepper

¼ teaspoon dried oregano

1 (24-ounce) jar marinara sauce, divided

2 tablespoons white wine

1 medium Chinese eggplant, sliced into ⅛-inch-thick rounds

4 cups shredded mozzarella cheese, divided

1½ cups (14 ounces) ricotta cheese

½ cup shredded Parmesan cheese, divided

1 large egg

2 tablespoons chopped fresh parsley, plus more to garnish

Freshly ground black pepper, for garnish

My daughter, Michaela, adores lasagna, but we're only a family of four—the large pans are just too much for us. But I can easily make eight of these roll-ups and I don't have to find room in the freezer for a gigantic amount of leftovers. It's easy, less work to cook, you don't have to buy as much to make it, and, best of all, it tastes just as good as regular lasagna. What's not to love? And if you're cooking for only two people, you can fit your rolls nicely into a bread pan. If you want to make the dish a tad healthier, try throwing in some spinach—you barely taste it.

1 • Preheat the oven to 375°F.

2 • Bring a large pot of salted water to a boil. Add the noodles and cook according to the package instructions, then drain and transfer them to a bowl of ice water to stop the cooking process.

3 • In a large skillet over medium-high heat, heat 2 tablespoons of the olive oil. Add the ground beef and cook, breaking up with a spatula, until no longer pink, about 2 minutes. Add the onion and cook, stirring, until softened, about 3 minutes. Add the garlic, ½ teaspoon of the salt, the white pepper, and the oregano and cook, stirring constantly, for 1 minute. Add 2 cups of the marinara sauce, bring to a simmer, and cook, stirring frequently, for 2 minutes. Then add the white wine and simmer over low heat, stirring frequently, for 5 minutes. Transfer the meat sauce to a bowl and set aside.

4 • Wash and dry the pan. Add the remaining 2 tablespoons olive oil and set over medium heat, then add the eggplant and cook, flipping often, until tender, about 5 minutes. Season with the remaining ½ teaspoon salt, then transfer the eggplant to a bowl and set aside.

5 • In a large bowl, stir together half of the mozzarella, the ricotta, ¼ cup of the Parmesan, the egg, and 2 tablespoons of the parsley.

(RECIPE CONTINUES)

6 • You're ready to assemble. Line a 9-by-11-inch casserole dish with parchment paper and spread a thin layer of marinara sauce on bottom. Lay a lasagna strip out flat and spread 3 tablespoons of the cheese mixture over the top. Add 2 tablespoons of the meat sauce on top of the cheese mixture. Then top with eggplant slices down the center in a single layer (about 6 slices). Top with about 1 tablespoon of mozzarella cheese and ½ tablespoon of Parmesan. Roll the noodles up with the ingredients inside like a roll cake. Insert a toothpick in the center through the entire roll and place it in casserole dish. Repeat for the remaining 7 rolls.

7 • Spread the remaining marinara sauce over the tops of the roll-ups and sprinkle the remaining mozzarella and Parmesan on top. Cover the dish with foil, making sure that the foil isn't touching the cheese.

8 • Bake, covered, for 35 minutes. Remove the foil and broil for 2 to 3 minutes, or until the cheese is lightly golden.

9 • To serve, using a spatula and a spoon, find the individual rolls, gently pick each one up, and plate. Garnish with the parsley and black pepper.

LION'S HEAD

PREP TIME: 10 MINUTES

COOK TIME: 20 MINUTES

SERVES: 4 TO 6

1 large egg, beaten

2 tablespoons light soy sauce

2 teaspoons dark mushroom soy sauce

2 cups plus ½ teaspoon corn oil, plus more for dredging, divided

3½ teaspoons cornstarch, divided

3 to 4 pinches kosher salt, divided

1½ pounds ground turkey

1 whole head of napa cabbage (sliced into 3-by-3-inch squares)

1 (14.5-ounce) can low-sodium chicken broth

2 to 3 pinches ground white pepper

Chopped scallions and cooked white rice (see page 236), for serving

The Chinese are very imaginative people—we use animals to represent our gods, our horoscopes, and even our personalities. It isn't surprising, then, that we get creative with our food, too. So why *is* it referred to as "lion's head" or, as my mother called it, "shizitou"? The meatballs, large in size, represent the lion's head, and the napa cabbage, surrounding the meatballs, is the lion's mane. Clever, right?

As a kid, this was my comfort food—my mother made it with juicy pork, and it was so delicious, warm and hearty and filling. Now that I make it for my family, I have subbed out the pork for ground turkey, making the dish healthier; the turkey also cooks faster and gives the meatballs a lighter density, so they're not sitting heavily in your stomach after dinner.

One of my greatest triumphs in life has been wooing my mother with my lion's head—she now prefers my ground turkey version to her pork version! Of course, being the typical Chinese mom, she still thinks I don't actually know how to cook. (SIGH!)

1 • In a large nonreactive bowl, use chopsticks to mix together the egg, light soy sauce, mushroom soy sauce, and ½ teaspoon of the corn oil. Sprinkle in 2 teaspoons of the cornstarch and a pinch of salt and mix well. Add the ground turkey and mix well with the seasoning.

2 • To make the meatballs, coat a plate in cornstarch. Prepare a bowl of water. Wet your hands lightly before grabbing a handful of meat mixture to prevent the meat from sticking to your hands. Toss the meat mixture back and forth between your palms to form the meat into six or seven 3-inch balls. Roll the meatballs on the plate to coat them with cornstarch.

(RECIPE CONTINUES)

3 • Add the remaining 2 cups of corn oil to a large wok, then heat the oil over high heat. Gently place the meatballs in the hot oil for a quick fry on all sides, turning them as they brown, until a deep golden-brown crust is formed, 1 to 2 minutes. The meat inside will not yet be fully cooked. Remove the meatballs from the wok and drain on paper towels. Turn off the heat.

4 • Remove bits of meat and residue from the hot oil with a mesh skimmer. Remove all but 2 to 3 tablespoons of the oil from the wok. The leftover oil can be used to cook other foods.

5 • Turn the heat to high. Add the cabbage and cook, stirring constantly, until soft but not wilted, about 3 minutes. Transfer half of the stir-fried napa cabbage into a large pot, placing larger pieces on the bottom. Add the meatballs on top of the cabbage. Then add the remaining cabbage on top of the meatballs.

6 • Set the pot over high heat, pour the chicken broth into the pot, and bring to a boil, about 5 minutes. Reduce the heat to medium-low, then simmer until the meatballs are cooked through, about 15 minutes. Season with 2 to 3 pinches of salt and white pepper.

7 • Make a slurry by stirring together the remaining 1½ teaspoons of cornstarch and 1 tablespoon water in a small bowl and mix it into the broth while the liquid is boiling to lightly thicken the sauce. Turn off the heat. Garnish with scallions and serve with rice.

SPAGHETTI AND MING MEATBALLS

PREP TIME: 15 MINUTES

COOK TIME: 30 MINUTES

SERVES: 4

FOR THE MEATBALLS:

1 pound lean ground turkey or beef

1 large egg

½ cup plain breadcrumbs

1 teaspoon garlic powder

1 teaspoon kosher salt

½ teaspoon paprika

½ teaspoon ground white pepper

2 tablespoons cornstarch

2 tablespoons olive oil

FOR THE SAUCE:

2 tablespoons olive oil

1 medium white or sweet onion, finely chopped

6 garlic cloves, minced

1 (24-ounce) jar marinara sauce

1¾ cups diced tomatoes

½ cup red wine

2 tablespoons tomato paste

1 tablespoon freshly grated Parmesan cheese, plus more for garnish (optional)

1 to 2 teaspoons sugar

1 teaspoon dried oregano

1 teaspoon dried basil

1 teaspoon garlic powder

½ teaspoon kosher salt

½ teaspoon ground cumin

¼ teaspoon freshly ground black pepper

Pinch chili powder

½ cup soy, oat, or regular milk

1 pound pasta of your choice, cooked per package instructions to al dente

This recipe is a staple in our home. It's an easy, hearty dish, and the sauce is so much better than any of the jarred stuff you might buy at the grocery store. (Although, I'll be honest, when I'm in a time crunch, I've been known to use jarred spaghetti sauce and a few extra ingredients to zhuzh it up.) I temper the acidity of my tomato sauce by adding a little milk. I also go easy on the herbs—just the basics, and not too much.

My son, Cooper, has even made it for his friends in college, which makes me a proud mama. Once you get the hang of making the meatballs, I suggest you double the recipe and make smaller ones and freeze them. They come in very handy for meatball sandwiches.

1 • MAKE THE MEATBALLS: In a large bowl, mix together the meat and egg. Mix in the breadcrumbs, garlic powder, salt, paprika, and white pepper.

2 • Wet your hands a little before you start forming the meatballs to help prevent sticking. Form palm-size (2-inch) meatballs, like you're making a snowball. Roll the packed meatballs lightly in cornstarch, just coating them.

3 • In a large skillet over medium-high, heat the olive oil. Add the meatballs and brown them on all sides, about 8 minutes total cooking time. Remove the skillet from the heat.

4 • MAKE THE SAUCE: In a medium saucepan over medium heat, heat the olive oil. Add the onion and cook, stirring constantly, until translucent, about 7 minutes. Add the garlic and cook, stirring constantly, until fragrant, about 1 minute. Add the marinara sauce, diced tomatoes, red wine, tomato paste, Parmesan, sugar, oregano, basil, garlic powder, salt, cumin, black pepper, and chili powder. Bring it to a boil over medium-high heat, stirring constantly to prevent the sauce from splattering out of the pot. Lower the heat to a simmer (or remove the pot from the heat if you're using an electric cooktop) and stir in the milk for creaminess. Add the meatballs. Simmer over low heat to thicken, about 15 minutes.

5 • Serve the sauce over your pasta of choice. Garnish with freshly grated Parmesan cheese and black pepper, if desired.

PREP TIME: 10 MINUTES

COOK TIME: 15 MINUTES

SERVES: 4

BACON FRIED RICE

5 large eggs

2 tablespoons plus 1 teaspoon vegetable oil, divided (or use the bacon grease)

2 teaspoons Shaoxing Chinese cooking wine

¼ teaspoon plus 1 pinch kosher salt, divided

¼ teaspoon plus 1 pinch ground white pepper, divided

8 ounces bacon, cut into 1-inch pieces

6 cups white rice, day-old or overnight (see page 236)

4 scallions, white and green parts, chopped

2 tablespoons light soy sauce

1 teaspoon dark mushroom soy sauce

½ tablespoon garlic powder

I play a lot of badass characters on screen, ones who know how to punch and kick and who seem pretty much invincible. Fennec Shand, for example? She's an assassin! But the real me? I have an Achilles' heel, and it's a doozy: bacon. But as much as I adore bacon, I've really only thought of it as an a.m. accessory, paired with eggs and toast. That changed one night when I had to whip up a quick dinner for my family. I had some leftover rice that I wanted to use for fried rice, but no protein to accompany it. I opened my fridge and stared in vain for something to use, not seeing anything until I had almost shut the door completely. Wait . . . bacon? Bacon makes everything taste better! Why not bacon fried rice? Bacon is really easy to cook in a wok, and instead of throwing out the grease I use it to further flavor the rice. This was an instant, very decadent hit. Just don't eat it every day—the cholesterol and saturated fat are admittedly not the healthiest.

Fried rice is one of the most versatile dishes out there, so think of this recipe as a template. You can substitute ground turkey, chicken, shrimp, or pork for the bacon. Vegetarian? Omit the meat and add extra veggies. I got creative in a pinch, and now it's your turn!

1 • In a small bowl, lightly beat the eggs with 1 teaspoon of water.

2 • In a large wok over medium-high heat, heat 1 teaspoon of the oil. Add the beaten eggs and cook, stirring, until half cooked, 2 to 3 minutes, then splash with the cooking wine. Season with a pinch of salt and white pepper. Remove the eggs from the wok and set aside. Wipe the wok clean with paper towels.

3 • In a different large wok or skillet over medium-high heat, cook the bacon, stirring frequently, until crispy, 6 to 8 minutes. Transfer to a paper towel–lined plate to absorb the excess grease. Set aside.

(RECIPE CONTINUES)

4 • Depending on your dietary restrictions for salt or fat intake, you can use the bacon grease; it will make for a tastier fried rice. Otherwise, remove the bacon grease and use vegetable oil instead. Add the remaining 2 tablespoons of oil or bacon grease to the first wok over high heat. Add the overnight rice and cook, stirring constantly—the overnight rice usually will be clumpy, so break up the clumps and cook for 2 minutes. Add the scallions, then stir in the light soy sauce and dark mushroom soy sauce. Continue to toss the rice with a spatula to make it fluffy and cook for 1 to 2 more minutes, adding more oil if needed. Add the eggs and bacon and cook, stirring constantly, until warmed through, about 30 seconds. Stir in the garlic powder, the remaining ¼ teaspoon of salt, and ¼ teaspoon of white pepper.

5 • Serve hot.

COOK'S NOTE: *Don't over-scramble the eggs; just lightly scramble them. It looks prettier when you can see the white and yellow. The white is fluffier when it cooks directly, and, overall, the eggs come out less dry. The cooking wine also helps to keep them fluffy!*

PREP TIME: 35 MINUTES
PLUS 2 HOURS MARINATING TIME

COOK TIME: N/A

SERVES: 2 TO 4

ASIAN SWEET PICKLED CUCUMBER SALAD

4 Persian cucumbers

¼ teaspoon kosher salt

2 tablespoons rice vinegar

1 tablespoon plus 1 teaspoon granulated sugar or sugar substitute

½ teaspoon sesame seeds, for garnish

Cucumber is used in savory, spicy, and even sweet dishes in Chinese cuisine. I first made this for my mother-in-law, Kitty, because she'd had it at a Chinese restaurant somewhere and loved it. Now every time she visits, I prepare it, because she says other places make it too sour or too sweet (but I make it just right!). She has developed dementia, but she always remembers this dish and happily eats it with breakfast, lunch, or dinner. She never gets sick of it! I like to think that food offers another pathway to the brain's memory center, and that's why she still knows this is one of her favorites. As her memory declines, it's nice to hold on to this small connection I have with her.

It's such a simple side dish, and super easy when using a mandoline to slice the cukes very thin—it's fun! Just be careful when you get close to the end of the cucumber as you slice; that thing is sharp.

1 • Thinly slice the cucumbers using a mandoline set to the thinnest setting or a very sharp knife.

2 • In a medium bowl, sprinkle the salt over the cucumbers and mix well by hand. Let it sit on the counter for 30 minutes to allow the water to seep out.

3 • Rinse the salt off the cucumbers and drain all the water. In a medium nonreactive bowl, add the vinegar and sugar and stir to combine. Add the cucumber and mix well. Refrigerate the cucumbers and let them marinate for 2 hours or more.

4 • Add more sugar if you find it's not sweet enough. To serve, remove the pickled cucumbers from the liquid and garnish with sesame seeds. Serve as a side dish.

DRAGON FRUIT CHEESECAKE CUPS

PREP TIME: 20 MINUTES PLUS 1 HOUR TO CHILL

COOK TIME: 50 MINUTES

MAKES 24 MINI CHEESECAKES

FOR THE JAM:

2 pink-fleshed dragon fruit, flesh scooped and finely chopped

2 tablespoons granulated sugar

1 tablespoon fresh lemon juice

FOR THE CHEESECAKES:

24 Nilla wafers

2 (8-ounce) packages cream cheese, room temperature

½ cup granulated sugar

2 large eggs, room temperature

1 teaspoon pure vanilla extract

My first official date with my husband was an epic picnic at a fairly isolated section of beach in Malibu. It made me slightly nervous when he pulled a large duffel bag out of the trunk in the parking lot. *If he pulls out a shovel*, I thought, *I'm going to scream and run.* To my relief, Eric pulled out a boombox instead. The New Yorker in me was on alert. After all, we'd known each other for only a couple of days. But we walked to a beautiful spot under the moon and the stars. He spread out a beach blanket on the soft sand and proceeded to set up a five-course meal. No guy had ever done that for me before! Dinner ended with these individual cupcake-size, cherry-filled pies. Needless to say, he won my heart. Here I swapped out the cherry for dragon fruit; both will win someone's heart.

1 • MAKE THE JAM: Add the dragon fruit to a medium saucepan over medium heat. Stir in the sugar. Bring to a simmer and, stirring frequently to prevent burning or sticking, cook until it reaches a jam-like consistency, 30 to 35 minutes. Stir in the lemon juice and cook, stirring frequently, to thicken, about 4 more minutes. Small chunks of the dragon fruit will remain; puree it if you prefer it smooth. Set aside to cool.

2 • Preheat the oven to 375°F.

3 • MAKE THE CHEESECAKES: Line the cups of two muffin pans (I have found that the double-lined foil and paper cupcake liners are best) and place a Nilla wafer in the bottom of each.

4 • In a bowl with an electric mixer, mix together the cream cheese, sugar, eggs, and vanilla until smooth and creamy. Evenly portion out the cheese mixture among the prepared muffin cups.

5 • Transfer the pan to the oven and bake for 15 to 18 minutes, or until the cheesecakes are a bit puffed up and the centers are not quite firm, as you don't want to overbake them. Set aside to cool.

6 • Divide dollops of the jam among the cooled cheesecakes, then cover and refrigerate for 1 hour or until ready to serve. Remove the outer foil cups and serve in the paper linings.

PANTRY FUNDAMENTALS

SRIRACHA HOT
NATURAL COLOR
PVC 不添加BPA
香 辣 脆
油 辣 椒
LAOGANMA
SPICY CHILI CRISP
NET WT:7.41OZ(210G)
淨含量：7.41盎司(210克)
香 李錦記 港
舊庄
特级蠔油
始創於1888年 • SINCE 1888
LEE KUM KEE'S
PREMIUM OYSTER SAUCE
NET WT. 18 oz (1 lb 2 oz) 510 g

PERFECT RICE

First things first. Let's talk about THE fundamental: rice. It should be easy to make, right? And, well, yeah, it is. But if you want to make *perfect* rice—and you should, as rice is a staple of Chinese food and accompanies so many of the dishes in this book—you need to pay attention to your grains. Otherwise, you might end up with mushy or burnt results. And nobody wants that. Ruined rice ruins meals. A little care will go a long way! Am I scaring you? Don't worry, you've got this. I know you do. I'm even giving you two methods, so if you don't have a rice cooker, don't panic—I've got you covered.

Here's what you need:

LONG-GRAIN WHITE RICE. My preference is jasmine because it's more fragrant and has a great texture and flavor. But really, any long-grain white rice will do.

You can use brown rice instead of white, but most Asians, and definitely this particular Chinese American, opt for white rice, even though it's been getting a bad reputation for spiking glucose levels. One way to make white rice spike less is to put cooked rice in the refrigerator or freezer overnight. This will make a more starch-resistant rice. But I've been eating it all my life and am doing just fine.

A VESSEL. Either a rice cooker or a medium-size pot.

WATER. I use the finger method for the water added. It seems to me that most Asians cook rice using this method, and I find it's the best way to make perfect rice every time! Alternatively, you can use equal parts water to rice.

And here's a beauty tip: After the second rice rinse, the drained water can be saved and used to wash your face and hair. It's a gentle cleanse and naturally adds softness—we don't waste a thing around here!

RICE COOKER METHOD

1 to 3 cups of jasmine or long-grain white rice

Water

1 • Add the rice to the inner pot, then pour in enough cold water to cover. Swirl the rice around with your hand to wash the starch off. The water will become cloudy. Drain and then repeat this rinsing process two more times until the water is almost clear. Drain.

2 • Pat the rice so that it is level in the pot. Place your index finger lightly on the top of the rice, then slowly fill the pot with water until it reaches the first line on your index finger, measuring in several locations.

3 • Place the pot in the rice cooker and follow your rice cooker instructions, usually about 40 minutes on the "quick cook" setting.

4 • Once the rice is cooked, let it sit for 5 to 10 minutes, then fluff it with a fork. Serve immediately or keep it warm in the cooker until ready to serve.

STOVETOP METHOD

1 to 3 cups of jasmine or long-grain white rice

Water

1 • Follow steps 1 and 2 of the rice cooker method using a small pot.

2 • Cook the water and rice over high heat until it comes to a boil. Lower the heat to medium-low and cover, placing chopsticks (or something similar) under the lid or leaving the lid slightly askew so that a little bit of steam can come out. Cook for 15 to 20 minutes or until the water is absorbed—you can eyeball it—without stirring the rice. (My mother says that when the steam starts curling, that's when the rice is done!)

3 • Remove the pot from the heat and remove the chopsticks so that the lid fits snugly. Let the rice sit for 5 to 10 minutes more.

4 • Fluff with a fork or rice spoon. It's best when served hot with food. Make sure to refrigerate any leftover rice in a covered container.

GETTING SAUCY WITH IT

If you open my fridge at any given moment, you'll find more sauces than space. Rows of bottles, jars, and pastes—some with labels half in Chinese, some half empty (but never thrown out, of course), and all essential. Growing up in a Chinese American household, these weren't "condiments"—they were building blocks. Tools. Shortcuts. Secrets.

Here's a little guide to a few of the condiments, sauces, and ingredients found in my pantry—and some other ways they can be used beyond this book. You might just find yourself deep in Ming-yvering mode, tweaking your own recipes with these flavors, as you get comfortable with them. Plus, if you ever find yourself standing in an Asian market aisle wondering "What on Earth do I do with this?" come back to this section or ask someone at the market. It can be daunting at first, but soon you'll be an expert on most of these items.

Light Soy Sauce

Lighter in color but saltier than dark soy, this is the everyday soy sauce used for stir-fries, marinades, dipping sauces, and anywhere you want a clean, savory flavor. It's bright and briny. I prefer Chinese soy sauce to Japanese.

Dark Soy Sauce

The moody older sibling—darker, thicker, and slightly sweet. It's more about color and depth than salt, and it's what is used to add that glossy, mahogany finish to red-cooked pork or braised tofu. Just a little goes a long way! And again, the Chinese dark soy is what I prefer.

Dark Mushroom Soy Sauce

Like dark soy sauce but with an earthy, umami-rich mushroom quality. This one's for when you want to enhance your sauces and gravies. Try it in noodle dishes or when braising veggies—it brings a subtle funk that makes people go, "Wait—what *is* that? It's amazing."

Oyster Sauce

No oysters were harmed in the making of this magical sauce (okay, maybe a few). Thick, sweet, salty, and savory, this sauce is a staple in Cantonese cooking. It adds a rich backbone to greens, beef, noodles—basically everything. It's like ketchup's more complex cousin.

Fish Sauce

Salty, funky, and loaded with depth, fish sauce smells intense but cooks up into pure umami gold. A dash goes a long way in stir-fries, soups, and even dumpling fillings. Don't smell it—just use it.

Black Bean Sauce

Made from fermented black soybeans, this chunky, salty-savory sauce is a flavor bomb in a jar. Use it in stir-fried beef, seafood, or eggplant dishes when you want that punchy, fermented funk. A little garlicky, a little salty, and deeply satisfying.

Doubanjiang (spicy bean paste)

This spicy, salty, fermented paste from Sichuan is what gives dishes like mapo tofu (see page 121 for my recipe) their signature fire and complexity. Made with broad beans, soybeans, and chili, it's the heart and soul of many spicy Chinese dishes. Proceed with love and a spoon.

Sriracha Aioli

Creamy, garlicky, and perfect as a dip for dumplings, a drizzle over rice bowls, or even spread on a spicy sandwich. Not traditional, but undeniably addictive.

Chili Crisp

Crunchy, savory, spicy, and just a little bit sweet—chili crisp is the life of the pantry party. Drizzle it over eggs, spoon it onto dumplings, or stir it into noodles. The crispy garlic and onion bits are half the fun.

Chili Sauce

Smooth and slightly sweet with just the right kick, this is your every-bite companion. It's great on dim sum, grilled meats, or stirred into fried rice. Think of it as ketchup for grown-ups who like a little heat.

Hot Chili Paste

Thicker and more intense than chili sauce, this paste packs serious punch. Great for marinades, soups, and any dish that needs a fiery backbone. Keep a glass of water nearby—but don't say I didn't warn you.

Spicy Chili Oil

This is liquid lava in the best way possible. Smoky, red-hot, and deeply flavorful, it adds instant pop to noodles, dumplings, or stir-fried greens. Just a drizzle will do . . . unless you're brave.

Chinkiang Vinegar

China's answer to balsamic—dark, tangy, and slightly sweet. This black vinegar adds brightness to dumpling sauces, cucumber salads, and braised dishes. Keep it on hand for when you want to cut through rich flavors with a little zip.

Shaoxing Chinese Cooking Wine

This amber-hued rice wine adds depth and aroma to stir-fries, soups, and braised dishes. A splash in a hot wok unlocks flavors like magic. Think of it as the secret whisper behind your favorite Chinese takeout.

S&B Golden Curry Powder

This Japanese-style curry powder has notes of turmeric, cumin, and warming spices, but with a mellow sweetness that makes it ultra-comforting. Add it to chicken or veggie stir-fries when you want a gentle curry vibe.

S&B Golden Curry Squares

These convenient little bricks melt into a savory-sweet, silky curry sauce. Great for lazy-day dinners, just toss them into a pot with meat, potatoes, and carrots.

PRE-PREP TIPS

Whether you're cooking for one, for date night, or for your whole big, hungry family, figuring out serving sizes can sometimes feel like . . . math. And not the fun kind. Well, is there fun in math other than, say, counting money? LOL. One thing I've learned the hard way? Don't wait until you're mid-cooking (and possibly mid-mess) to start measuring out a bunch of spices.

Here's a little trick I picked up: pre-prep the dry stuff! You know those tiny takeout sauce containers? Grab a few online—or reuse the glass spice jars you've been meaning to toss (just clean them first!). I label mine with painter's tape and a Sharpie so I know exactly what dish they're for.

Ultimately, you should learn to cook with your eyes and be able to measure intuitively, which will make cooking more enjoyable. So when you're just beginning to learn a new dish, see what a teaspoon of salt or a tablespoon of soy sauce looks like when it's poured from the bottle. Teach yourself to sense the amount.

But no matter how you cook, always know how many people you're cooking for, then add one more. I'd rather have too much food than leave someone hungry. Measure out your spices based on the head count and stash all the ones that go into the pan at the same time in one container. Boom—spice mix ready to go.

Restaurants actually do this all the time with sauces and broths, so if you're even *slightly* a planner (I try, okay?), it's worth doing that, too. It makes cooking feel a whole lot smoother—and way less like a scene from a cooking blooper reel.

Trust me, when it's time to make dinner, you'll be so glad Past You had their act together.

ACKNOWLEDGMENTS

To tell you the truth, I procrastinated with this section of the book—not because I lacked gratitude but because I felt overwhelmed by the fact that so many incredible people helped to make this book a reality. There aren't enough words to express my appreciation for all their time, energy, talent, and attention. They made this restaurant daughter believe she was someone worthy of having her own cookbook.

Thank you to my devoted fans, who have been demanding my recipes for *years*. I adore you all. I hope you love this book and that the wait was worth it!

Big thanks to Mommy and Baba for all the sacrifices you made in raising Jonathan, Lang, and me. You showered us with love through every delicious meal you cooked. And even though you are no longer with us, Baba, your recipes will live on for generations to come.

My biggest thank-you to my darling husband, Eric, and our two beautiful children, Michaela and Cooper; you are my absolute joys in life. Eric, you have always and unfailingly supported me, including in the madness of making this book. Kids, you've given me the best gig ever as your mom. I love you to the moon and back.

Thank you to Jonathan and Lang for all the memories. I'm grateful for the laughs and stories that only we understand. Love you guys for always being there for me!

A special shout-out to all the wonderful friends and family who have brought meaning to my life. Thank you for all the feasts we've shared together over the years.

Thanks to my wonderful managers Erik Kritzer and Ryan Bundra, along with Rami Qarooni, at LINK Entertainment. Your guidance was instrumental in turning this actress into an author. I'm so grateful to you for pushing me to look outside the box for new creative outlets.

Thanks to my talented literary agent, Katherine Latshaw at Folio Literary Management. With your unrelenting optimism and immense patience, you gave me the confidence to put my heart and soul into this book. Thank you for being my shifu, my mentor, and my friend.

A very sincere thank you to my editor, Justin Schwartz, for wholeheartedly believing in this book from the beginning. Your advocacy and enthusiasm drove me to do my very best even when I doubted myself. Thank you as well to Gina Navaroli, Richard Rhorer, and the entire Simon Element team for honoring my stories and recipes.

Thanks to Ann Volkwein for elevating my voice. Your invaluable contributions helped carry this book to the finish line, and your finesse with recipes was awe-inspiring.

Thank you to photographer Jennifer Chong; I'm grateful for your sharp eye. Your incredible team—Jessica Darakjian, Caroline Hwang, David K. Peng, and Audrey Taylor, along with Laura Adkins, Caroline Benitez, and Ashli Buts—turned my home upside down with ingredients, equipment, and props, and I couldn't have been happier. Best house party ever!

Lots of love to my beautiful friend Suzanna M. Turner for your immense skill in glamming me up. Love you, sis!

Thank you, too, to Chaz Dean for the gorgeous haircut and color. I cherish your friendship.

Many thanks to my assistant, Lauren de Miranda, for your bubbly personality, your positivity, and your willingness to help; you were on top of everything.

A special thank-you to my friend Dennis Kwan for taking such fabulous photos of my family. You are an angel, Dennis.

Thank you to every person who works in the food industry. Whether you are farmers, ranchers, fishermen, chefs, restaurant workers, or delivery people, you all deserve our greatest respect and appreciation for ensuring that we have food on our tables.

Once more, I must give thanks to the love of my life, Eric. I'm the luckiest person to have you as my partner, both in life and in the kitchen. (You know, he's actually a damn good cook himself!) You are my knight in shining armor, my handsome leading man in the most romantic C-drama ever. I love you always.

INDEX

D

E

F

G

R

S

T

SIMON
ELEMENT

An Imprint of Simon & Schuster, LLC
1230 Avenue of the Americas
New York, NY 10020

Food Stylist: Caroline Hwang
Prop Stylist: Audrey Taylor
Photography Assistant: David K. Peng
Food Stylist Assistant: Jessica Darakjian
Prop Styling Assistants: Laura Adkins Jean, Ashli Buts, and Caroline Benitez

First Simon Element hardcover edition October 2026

SIMON ELEMENT and colophon are registered trademarks of Simon & Schuster, LLC

Interior design by Karla Schweer

Manufactured in Malaysia

10 9 8 7 6 5 4 3 2 1

Library of Congress Control Number: 2025946201

ISBN 978-1-6680-1161-4
ISBN 978-1-6680-1162-1 (ebook)